[contributors]

Landscapes of [Sub]stance

creative directors
Ashley Braquet
Leonardo Robleto Costante
Eduardo Santamaria Ruvalcaba

authors
Anneliza Carmalt Kaufer
Diana Gruberg
Claire Hoch
Joanna Karaman
Youngsoo Kim
Janet Lee
Kuhn Lee
Suzanne Mahoney
Alyssa Olson
Anooshey Rahim
Michael Shafir
Ian Sinclair
Autumn Visconti
Matthew Wiener

photography
Barrett Doherty

faculty advisors
Richard J Weller
Tatum Hands

[foreword]

Students of Landscape Architecture: 1914–2014

For 100 years since the first lectures in landscape architecture were delivered at Penn by George Burnap, students have been asking "how can we make this world better?" The extraordinary history of landscape architecture at the School of Design at the University of Pennsylvania is typically one told through the achievements of the department Chairs and faculty. McHarg, Spirn, Hunt, Olin and Corner are each luminaries of the field, but what is often overlooked is that their ideas and methods were developed in collaboration with students. Students have always been there: interpreting, testing and questioning their mentors. Students have provided the essential and critical feedback for the development of the discipline that Penn is associated with. Students have also been the ones who have taken these influences out beyond the shelter of the school into the complex reality of the world and shaped the profession as we know it.

Contributing their voices to Penn landscape architecture's centenary, Landscapes of [Sub]stance was written and produced entirely by current students. The creative directors of this project—Leo Robleto Costante, Ashley Braquet and Eduardo Santamaria—have led the project from start to finish with the vision and determination that characterizes the school. What follows is a fascinating insight into what Penn landscape architecture students are thinking now.

Richard J Weller
Martin and Margy Meyerson Chair of Urbanism
Professor and Chair of Landscape Architecture
The University of Pennsylvania

4

[contents]

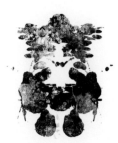

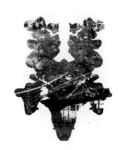
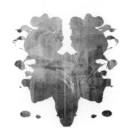

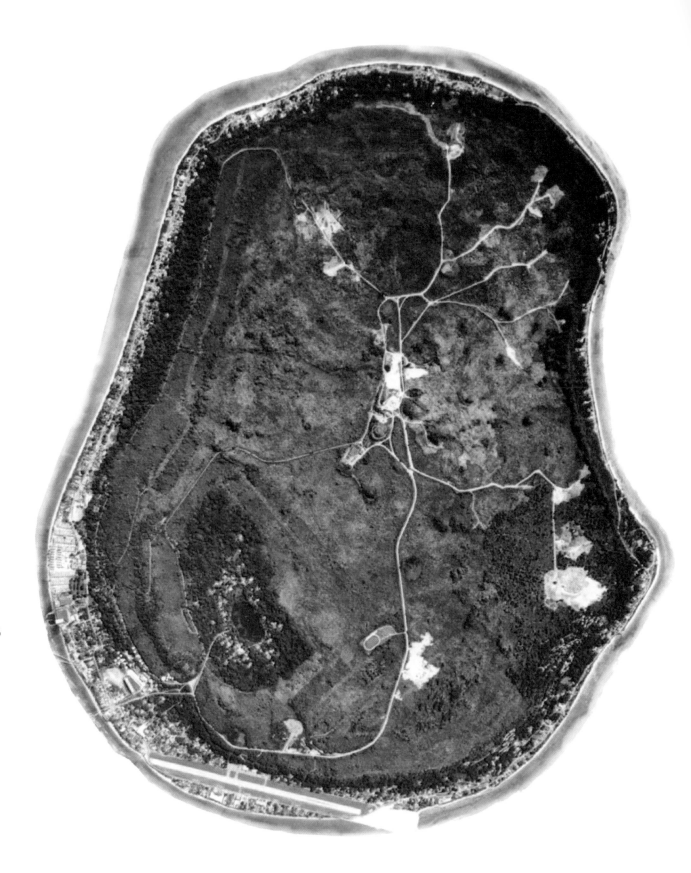

What is this world we have created for ourselves? Through continuous transformation, manipulation and globalization, it seems we have ultimately changed it all. We are only just beginning to understand the consequences of these changes. Like Rorschach stains, meaning and potential lies within them, waiting to be revealed.

Take the example of Nauru, a small once paradisiacal island in the Pacific that offers a dystopian warning: ignore landscape and suffer the consequences. Few places in the world exhibit such a unique range of problems that originate from the interaction between people and landscape.

Once the nation with one of the highest GDPs in the world, Nauru has been carelessly turned into an emergency flotation device. Phosphate mining once gave the country prosperity, but continuous exploitation of its rich landscape and failure to restore the balance with nature has left the island at an ecological point of no return. The transformation of "Pleasant Island" into an inhospitable rock has left Nauru with no agriculture, little biodiversity, an unhealthy society and a crumbling economy.

A drive around the island offers a glimpse of how important landscapes will become to the survival of any society and culture. Extinct mining activities have deemed 80% of the island's surface area uninhabitable. The removal of vegetation for mining has created a heat dome that pushes rainfall away from its coasts, eliminating the potential for reforestation and cultivation. The island's economy currently relies on fishing permits and internment for refugees seeking asylum, while all of Nauru's food is imported, making the population one of the most obese and diabetes-ridden in the world. Add to this impending sea level rise and Nauru might very well be the prologue of what the world will face at larger scales.

Landscapes of [Sub]stance

In Landscapes of [Sub]stance we asked Penn students what landscape architects can do in the face of the big issues that this world of our own making now presents. Consequently you will find articles on big issues, such as food, energy and waste, among others. As a whole the articles show a certain apprehension toward what the world has become: a combination of awe and disgust. But from within this ambivalence is a discernible willingness to engage both with ideas and matter, and to do so without sentimentality, without hubris, without salvation.

When do we let go? More importantly, when do we wrangle it back? Claire Hoch frames an aesthetic sensibility of a new type of 'wilderness' in uncertain landscapes prevalent and endemic in contemporary times.

[wild]

Dirty Stinkin' Wilds: Experimenting with Uncertainty
Claire Hoch

"Refinement of matter from one state to another does not mean that so called impurities of sediment are bad- the earth is built on sedimentation and disruption."

-Robert Smithson[1]

What do we make of the wilds? The wildernesses of the world, particularly in developed nations, are parceled and preserved; but what about the wilds — the unsanctioned and un-designed? Many of the world's wilds are protected by the sheer geologic impossibility of large-scale development, climatic impediments to human occupation, and the lack of known resources available for extraction. Newer wilds are developing on abandoned extraction sites surrounding our cities in areas once rich with mineral deposits and biodiversity, now teaming with hardy pioneers (both arboreal and human). Generally considered a biological hazard and peri-urban blight, this wild is defined by the processes it undergoes, not the established beauty it contains. And yet these places can be beautiful. Throughout its history, landscape architecture has always manipulated natural systems towards idealized ends. This article explores the possibility of relinquishing idealized aesthetics and accepting the dirty, the ugly and the entropic. It examines the degree to which design can engage these 'unsightly' qualities without itself dissolving into invisibility.

The Pristine

As a proxy for nature, wilderness is never just culture's naive inverse. Wild is a term deeply embedded in the American psyche. In his book *Wilderness and the American Mind*, Roderick Nash argues that America built the foundation of its identity on the vastness of its untamed landscape.[2] The early American politician and naturalist DeWitt Clinton exclaimed in an address to the American Academy of Art, "Can there be a country in the world better calculated than ours to exercise and to exalt the imagination — to call into activity the creative powers of the mind, and to afford just views of the beautiful, the wonderful, and the sublime?"[3] The early American wilderness quickly came to stand as the antithesis of the over-cultivated landscapes of Europe. Paradoxically, these wildernesses were constructed and aestheticized in the national imagination through the application of the British landscape aesthetics they supposedly transcended. The idealized beauty of these places was discriminatory insofar as a particular aesthetic of pure nature was used to justify the removal of both predators and Native American 'savages' from lands beyond the city.[4] The wild was to be preserved and maintained for its untapped instrumental and idealized values: for the sustained use of natural resources, for its recreational purposes and for the beauty and spiritual experience it provided to the trained aesthetic of the urban elite.

As the conservation movement evolved through the preservationist thinking of Thoreau, Muir and Leopold, America's relationship with the wild started to expand beyond the worth of its available resources to an appreciation of the intrinsic value of nature, leading to more stringent regulations on protected wilderness lands. The revered father of American landscape architecture Frederick Law Olmsted was a preeminent figure in the formation of a legally protected American wilderness. In 1864, Olmsted chaired the congressional commission which proclaimed Yosemite as America's first National Park. Olmsted predicted the necessary construction and maintenance of a landscape that would need to accommodate millions of visitors each year.[5] A 2013 plan for the Merced River drawn up by the National Park Service calls for the restoration of disturbed meadows and a significant reduction of human presence in Yosemite National Park.[6] This plan is a significant advance in recognizing the importance and agency of natural ecosystems and processes, yet manages to maintain the myth of a pristine wilderness — a nature separate from humanity. It ignores the myriad benefits that novel ecosystems offer and the ability of natural systems to evolve with human dynamics.

The Dirty

Today America's preserved wildernesses are dwarfed in number by the new wilds developing on the very landscapes that were once used for the extraction of their resources. These new wilds differ from wilderness. These are the untidy, ignored spaces we have all bypassed: the forgotten spaces of industry, derelict farms, leftover spaces along rails and highways, and the pits and piles of the high-speed geomorphology of the Anthropocene. Architect Ignasi de Sola-Morales Rubio's seminal text on the Terrain Vague describes these places as "Void, absence, yet also promise, the space of the possible, of expectation."[7] Morales stresses the importance of not erasing these vague places and urges the design professions to engage dialectically with their qualities. The dialectic at the heart of the wild is on the one hand its inextricable link to humans and on the other its absolute unfamiliarity. The wilds provide a future unknown to our imagination. Like the abject, the new wilds subvert progress. As such, in a world now entirely dominated by human development they are important both biologically and allegorically. As Julia Kristeva explains, "The time of abjection is double: a time of oblivion and thunder, of veiled infinity and the moment when revelation bursts forth."[8] But this revelation is very often unwanted and avoided; it forces us to face the consequences of our actions and question the roots of our global enterprise.

The wilds are not National Parks; they are wastelands, abject orifices either ignored or wiped clean and developed. Serving once as sources for urban development, or the spaces in between, pure conservationists see these wilds as appalling aberrations: toxic, eutrophic, feral, and unnatural. For the design professions and their clients, these sites are development opportunities and the narrative is always one of 'improvement'. Landscape architects go to work eagerly reclaiming, reinstating, rehabilitating, recovering, revegetating and ultimately redeeming. If left to their own devices, however, the wilds naturally evolve through succession to reach various states of ecological diversity and resilience. In other words, for zero input they offer maximum return. And yet the American environmental aesthetic and landscape architecture along with it has failed to see the value in these places as they are.

Anthropologist Mary Douglas and cultural critic Lewis Hyde offer a particularly potent analysis of the importance of the dirty in society as that which has no place.[9] "Dirt is always a product of creating order. And where there is dirt, there is always a system of some kind, and rules about dirt are meant to preserve that system."[10] Without dirt, we lose the ability to remember the residual impact of the rules that govern unfettered growth and consumption. That reminder is a necessary element of a self-reflective society, a society capable of adapting to the loss of habitat and depletion of resources, to climate change and rising sea levels. This dirt, our industrial residue and the wilds it bears, tells the story of urban growth, consumption, and waste, and its impacts on our planet.

In her essay *Uncertain Parks: Disturbed Sites, Citizens, and Risk Society,* landscape theorist Elizabeth Meyer describes the loss associated with the design aesthetic of many disturbed sites-turned-parks, "Large pastoral parks with ball fields and picnic shelters are more a form of amnesia, a practice of forgetting site histories, than indices of regional character and identity."[11] Wiping away the dirt through the blanket effect of greening efforts and pastoral design aesthetics conceals the identity and evolution of a place. It covers over the true impact of an industrial legacy on the identity of small towns and cities. It renders landscapes as static rather than dynamic and changing.

Maintaining Uncertainty or Can Design be Wild?

Designed landscapes can maintain uncertain, dynamic futures. This uncertainty is not solely addressed by a catalytic spark designed to accommodate projected use and unforeseen conditions, but may also be the result of a potentially ongoing and changing engagement and rebuilding process. While market limitations rarely allow for landscape firms to engage in ongoing design and management past the initial construction phase, these landscapes do exist. Anita Berrizbeitia describes Amsterdam's Bos as a highly managed yet dynamic park, one where "aspects of place are revealed" through selectively deciding what is to remain open-ended[12] Forestry management principles, similar to those designed by Olmsted for Central Park, are deployed to foster slow growing ash, maple, oak, and beech trees.

It is through the ongoing seeding and culling of pioneer vegetation that a later stage successional forest is able to grow without the expensive and risky planting of mature specimens. Process here is as ecological as it is an aesthetic, stimulating "a subjective engagement with landscape, one that is renewed as changes in color, texture, spatiality, and scents unfold through the seasons and, over the long term, through the changes brought on by the landscape's growth and decay."[13]

Ironically enough, it is often the designed management practices of the gardener, the farmer, and the forester— those continually engaged with the processes of nature— that are best able to accommodate and foster a wild and dynamic place. "The garden is a somewhat unruly extension of the human genome,"[14] says biologist Daniel Janzen whose phrase the 'gardenification of nature' refers to the necessity of novel management practices for a planet universally impacted by human growth and landscape manipulation. Through his experimental project, Area de Conservacion Guanacaste in Costa Rica, he has long embraced the navigation of political, social and biological processes in managing the diversity and lifespan of wildlands and degraded landscapes. In a 1998 collaboration with Del Oro S.A., an industrial citrus grower, Janzen was able to restore a strategically chosen pasture back to rainforest through the spreading of 300 tons of orange pulp onto non-native grasses. The Supreme Court declared the contract illegal, after a competitor sued Del Oro for dumping waste in a national park.[15] Although the project was biologically successful, the argument for the idealized aesthetic of a pure, untouched nature easily thwarted the innovative landscape efforts.

Landscapes that privilege management strategies over projected master plans allow material engagement and process to inform their ongoing life. The Oostvarderplassen is such a landscape. The nature reserve grew out of industrial dregs and maintains its changing form through introduced foraging horses and cattle. In 1932, Dutch engineers cut off a portion of the North Sea to form a freshwater lake and drained it 30 years later in preparation for industrial development. The ecologist Frans Vera adopted the highly artificial site (now 14 feet below sea level) after observing that thousands of graylag geese had changed the ecology of the marshy landscape to a mix of open water and reeds through their grazing patterns over a number of years before development began.[16] Embracing the site's management and construction, nature writer Emma Marris describes the landscape as one of the wildest places in Western Europe: "Life and death are plainly on display here, and there is plenty of each."[17] This landscape cannot be staged in its ideal realization because it inherently never reaches climax.

Elizabeth Meyer describes the aesthetic experience of the past as primarily visual, noting that a contemporary sublime can now be found through the experience of deep time rather than vast space.[18] She, along with Catherine Howett, Anne Whiston Spirn, and Yuriko Saito argue that an appreciation for the aesthetic in landscape architecture must be revived through the celebration of dynamic processes experienced "poly-sensually" and over time rather than through static scenery.[19] In her manifesto *Sustaining Beauty*, Meyer contends that the aesthetic experience is lacking in a contemporary practice focused on the performative functions of sustainable design. She argues that the power of a true aestheticism performs at the level of a highly perceptual and visceral experience, having the uncomfortable power to transform the way we think about landscapes in relation to energy and consumption.[20] Dirt (not just the stuff on the ground, but pollutants, debris, uncultivated vegetation, material decay, and societal accidents) may be ugly and uncomfortable, but that is to call it a transformative aesthetic experience on par with its opposite, beauty. Dirt is capable of scaring, surprising and awing us.

Feeling Small or Why to Let Go

The wilds are particularly uncomfortable for designers trained to improve problematic and disturbed sites. The rawness of unintended residue has a sensual power rarely met by designed landscapes. Retired sites of resource extraction offer the possibility for individuals to experience the raw power of an awesome geologic manipulation that rivals the sublime wilderness described by the European Romantics and early American settlers. Rob Wilson offers an interpretation of the contemporary sublime as a similarly ambivalent force, a re-imagined vision of bigness and power where, "shifting configurations of American grandeur remains one of awe-struck credulity with God, or that equally vast source of American infinitude reified into global power, 'Capital'".[21]

The power of this sublime wild is not only seen in the massive holes of exposed bedrock, but in the thriving monocultures of aspens and locusts colonizing extraction sites; it is seen in a globalized economy that depends upon the excavation of countrysides, the workers of its small towns, and the mega-infrastructures that mobilize it globally; it is found in the names of the proud counties in which these mines are dug, in the museums and bronze monuments that sprinkle their towns.

> "All of the site's histories—natural, social and industrial—are that landscape's voice...The industrial traces one finds, considered detritus by some, contain the memories, the story of that place. Keeping them is not about some romantic or nostalgic notion. Instead, their presence, along with new layers of interpretation and occupation, allows the evolution of the site histories to continue and for a community's association with that place to stay alive."
>
> -Julie Bargmann[22]

Coal Township is nestled along the Appalachian mountain range in eastern Pennsylvania's anthracite coal mining region. A satellite survey of the township presents over 25 mines in the immediate vicinity of the patch town Shamokin, home to roughly 7,000 residents. These mines are mostly abandoned, though some have been converted to aggregate quarries in the past few decades. The coal region stretches through at least seven counties of eastern Pennsylvania and contains hundreds of 'black diamond' pits along with their corresponding and unavoidably visible mountains of slag that extend the ridge line of the Appalachians. These landscapes are a hybrid human-nature geology.

The exposure and displacement of bedrock offers a profound view of the large-scale geologic and industrial manipulation that formed it. The new wilds of these mines and heaps are un-before scenes of tectonic motion in fast-forward, now undergoing momentous ecological transformation. The dirt and barrenness of the Pennsylvania mines created by the geologic process of sedimentation and the reversed industrial processes of digging, sorting and spoiling reveal uncomfortable scales of time. In such places one is enveloped by the vastness of space and time. The experience of smallness is a humbling and powerful one that reframes people as only one of many agents in a landscape's remaking.

The creative and ecologic agency of the spontaneous succession that occurs in these abandoned mine sites, also found in the managed reserves, provides not only the aesthetic experience of imagining the unknown, but also valuable ecosystem services. Ecologists today are reconsidering the role of traditional reclamation methods when dealing with abandoned mine sites. In a 2013 study out of the Czech Republic, coal spoils left to spontaneous vegetation, unlike those covered with fresh topsoil, were shown to offer significant habitat to a number of endangered vascular plants, correlating positively with the population of locally threatened Lepidoptera (the order contained moths and butterflies).[23] The primary succession resulting from years of heavy disturbance and continued minor disturbances (vehicular and pedestrian traffic and additional excavation) effectively maintained a markedly different and heterogeneous landscape.[24] Primary succession, once regulated by natural disturbance cycles is a significant component of a healthy ecosystem, affecting community health at every trophic level. This patch ecology, when stationed amidst forest or the urban grid offers myriad benefits for species whose rangelands are now encroached upon by urban development. The connection of these sites across a larger territory provides the possibility of the movement of plants and people together.

Revising Good Looks or What's a Designer to Do?

"Plants travel. Especially the herbs. They move in silence, like the wind. Nothing can be done about the wind. Were we to harvest the clouds, we would be surprised to find unpredictable seeds mixed with loess, fertile silt. Unthinkable landscapes are already being designed in the sky."

-Gilles Clement[25]

Although I am arguing for a greater appreciation of time and succession as a self-organizing phenomena, I do not mean to render the designer obsolete. I am suggesting we move beyond the permanent 'improvement' of landscapes to a more temporal practice, providing experimental, materially engaging, and accessible models for future landscape intervention. Small, location-specific experiments can be undertaken by designers in conjunction with advanced scientific modeling and monitoring programs to assess and explore novel ecologies.

As Anne Whiston Spirn states in *The Authority of Nature,* "The emphasis should be on a spirit of inquiry and exploration rather than close-minded certainty."[26]

The seeming emptiness of primary succession has long been regarded as unworthy of aesthetic appreciation. John R. Stilgoe argues that into the 19th century, the American classification of "good land" was held exclusively for land fit for agriculture. As the geological sciences developed, a dislike of barren lands increased as the speculation of the age of rocks and fossils challenged the legitimacy of the Bible's history of the earth.[27] As such, disturbed, barren lands may be suitable for resource extraction, but certainly not an aesthetic and spiritual experience. But as our landscapes are subsumed by accelerating extraction and disposal, we have a choice to make: reserve beauty to the last remaining vestiges of seemingly pure and healthy landscapes and the total aesthetic and ecological rehaul of newly designed landscapes or find value in the dirt.

The dirt is only growing.

References

1 Robert Smithson, "A Sedimentation of the Mind: Earth Projects" in Robert Smithson: The Collected Writings, ed. Jack Flam. (Berkeley: University of California Press, 1996). Originally published in Art Forum 7 (September 1968): 106.

2 Roderick Frazier Nash, Wilderness and the American Mind, 4th edition (New Haven: Yale University Press, 2001).

3 Ibid., 70 quoting from Thomas S. Cummings, Historic Annals of the National Academy of Design (Philadelphia, 1865) p. 12.

4 Donald Worster, Nature's Economy: A History of Ecological Ideas (Cambridge: Cambridge University Press, 1977): 265.

5 Anne Whiston Spirn, "Constructing Nature: The Legacy of Frederick Law Olmsted" in Uncommon Ground: Rethinking the Human Place in Nature, ed. William Cronon (New York: W.W. Norton and Company, 1996): 92.

6 Norimitsu Onishi, "A Plan to Save Yosemite by Curbing its Visitors," The New York Times, July 28, 2013, accessed August 3, 2013. http://www.nytimes.com/2013/07/29/us/plan-for-yosemite-calls-for-scaling-back-human-activity.html?pagewanted=all&_r=0

7 Ignasi de Sola-Morales Rubio, "Terrain Vague." in Anyplace, ed. Cynthia Davidson (Cambridge: MIT Press, 1995): 118–23.

8 Julia Kristeva, Powers of Horror: An Essay on Abjection, trans. Leon S Roudiez (New York: Columbia University Press, 1982): 9.

9 Mary Douglas, Purity and Danger: An Analysis of Concepts of Pollution and Taboo (London: Routledge and Kegan Paul, 1966).

10 Lewis Hyde, Tricker Makes This World: Mischief, Myth, and Art (New York: Farrar, Straus, and Ciroux, 2010): 176.

11 Elizabeth Meyer, "Uncertain Parks: Disturbed Sites, Citizens, and Risk Society," in Large Parks, ed. Julia Czerniak and George Hargreaves (New York: Princeton Architectural Press, 2007): 62.

12 Anita Berrezbietia, "Re-Placing Process" in Large Parks, ed. Julia Czerniak and George Hargreaves (New York: Princeton Architectural Press, 2007): 185.

13 Ibid., 177.

14 Daniel Janzen, "Gardenification of Wildland Nature and The Human Footprint," Science, Vol. 279. (1998).

15 Daniel Janzen, "Costa Rica's Area de Conservacion Guanacaste: A long march to survival through non-damaging biodevelopment," Biodiversity, Vol 1, No. 2, (2000): 13–14.

16 Emma Marris, Rambunctious Garden: Saving Nature in a Post-Wild World (New York: Bloomsbury USA, 2011): 67.

17 Ibid., 70.

18 Elizabeth Meyer, "Siezed by Sublime Sentiments: Between Terra Firma and Terra Incognita," in Richard Haag: Bloedel Reserve and Gas Works Park, ed. William S. Saunders (New York: Princeton Architectural Press, 1998): 6–28.

19 Catherine Howett, "Systems, Signs, Sensibilities: Sources for a New Landscape Aesthetic," Landscape Journal, Vol. 6. No. 1 (1987): 1-12; Anne Whiston Spirn, "The Poetics of City and Nature: Towards a New Aesthetic for Urban Design," Landscape Journal, Vol. 7. No. 2. (1988): 108–26; Yuriko Saito, "The Aesthetics of Unscenic Nature," The Journal of Aesthetics and Art Criticism, 56:2 (2013): 101–11.

20 Elizabeth Meyer, "Sustaining Beauty. The Performance of Appearance: A Manifesto in Three Parts," Journal of Landscape Architecture, 5 (2008): 6–23.

21 Rob Wilson, "The Postmodern Sublime: Local Definitions, Global Deformations of the US National Imaginary," American Studies, Vol. 43, No. 5 (1998): 518.

22 Julie Bargmann, interview by Jenna McKnight, GreenSource, October, 2007.

23 Robert Tropek, et al., "Local and Landscape Factors Affecting Communities of Plants and Diurnal Lepidoptera in Black Coal Spoil Heaps: Implications for Restoration Management," Ecological Engineering, 57 (2013): 252–260.

24 Ibid.

25 Gilles Clement, "The Garden in Movement 3," in Planetary Gardens: The Landscape Architecture of Gilles Clement, ed. Alessandro Rocco (Basel: Birkhauser, 2007): 17.

26 Anne Whiston Spirn, "The Authority of Nature: Conflict and Confusion in Landscape Architecture," in Nature and Ideology: Natural Garden Design in the Twentieth Century, ed. Joachim Wolschke-Bulmahn (Washington DC: Dumbarton Oaks Research Library and Collection, 1997): 260–261.

27 John R. Stilgoe, "Fair Fields and Blasted Rock: American Land Classification Systems and Landscape Aesthetics," American Studies, Vol. 22, No. 1 (1981): 21–33.

The Ogallala Aquifer is the source that ensures productivity in the American High Plains. Matthew Wiener searches for a new way to visualize unseen waters.

[reveal]

Grounding Water
Matthew Wiener

With water, we often fixate upon the sky and the surface. Conveyed as rain, storm, ocean, rise, river, and flood, water in these horizons is tactile; it can be tasted, felt, and seen.   Awash with such abundance and visibility, we have grown complacent in our representation of both the beauty these waters inspire and the threats they impose. There are, however, waters that elude our common senses, particularly those that are below—and dissolved within—the earth. Though they are substantially concealed, these elemental hybrids support vast agricultural and urban landscapes. Groundwater is seen as limitless because it is rarely seen at all.

If groundwater is invisible, representation must become the eyes and imagination of an increasingly myopic surface settlement. But, can an element of landscape as complex as groundwater be seen? Or drawn? What, if any, is the unique ability of the landscape architect in this pursuit? Can it add to that of the geologist? Or engineer? Or poet? Admittedly, many of the contemporary crises surrounding groundwater, in addition to myriad other complicated ecological and urban systems, are the result of failures to steward and conserve our natural environment. However, this article suggests an alternative to characterizations of groundwater as a resource in a state of abundance or depletion. It also challenges conventional landscape representation in the construction of this myth. Ultimately, it is an over-simplification to consider groundwater as an environmental *problem* that needs to be solved. The more difficult task, and the potential place of the designer, is to represent groundwater as a thing that needs to be seen.

By most standards, the Ogallala Aquifer (also known as the High Plains Aquifer) is shallow – the water table is 33 meters below the surface throughout roughly half the aquifer's range.[1] Its saturated thickness—a measure of the distance from the top of the water table to the base of the aquifer—ranges from 15 to 365 meters. Even so, the Ogallala is roughly 450,000 square kilometers in size and underlies eight states. It is thought to store one million billion gallons: a volume of water vast enough to cover the entire lower United States by 0.61 meters.[2,3]
"Fossil" waters contained within the Ogallala were

charged slowly throughout the Miocene epoch (23.03–5.332 million years ago) during a period when the High Plains was considerably warmer and wetter than it is today. Nascent materials throughout the region absorbed precipitation, atmospheric moisture and the residue of ancestral oceans, and then held it throughout the ages. Today, this stratigraphic layer consists of sands, unconsolidated gravels, and poorly silted clays, which vary considerably in their porosity and hydraulic conductivity. As a geologic unit it is referred to as the Ogallala formation, while locally it is known by pseudonyms including "Ash Hollow," "Sidney Gravel," and "Valentine".[4]

The Ogallala is not a static system, though it is certainly slow. Generally, groundwater flows through the aquifer in an easterly and downslope direction from the Rocky Mountains at a rate of approximately 0.3 m per day.[5] A raindrop that falls in Lake Itasca, at the headwaters of the Mississippi River, could reach the Gulf of Mexico in less than 90 days.[6] A raindrop falling at the northernmost point of the Ogallala in South Dakota (assuming a linear path and a regular rate of laminar flow) might arrive in central Texas after more than 3,500 years.[7]   Groundwater's latency is a result of its microscopic trickle through the interstices of geological formations. In contrast to surface water, which is seen to move rapidly over land in a line, groundwater passes slowly through it as a field.

The Ogallala is described in the science as both unconfined (meaning it is recharged through surface infiltration) and discontinuous. This latter categorization indicates that the aquifer is neither contiguous nor homogeneous. Rather, aquitards, non-porous substrates and inhibitory geological features have created a lithic patchwork of deep and shallow pockets where water is enmeshed in ground. In essence, the aquifer is neither consistently wet nor dry. Instead, it is a fluid gradient; wells in the Ogallala may gush over three thousand liters per minute, or increasingly, may yield nothing at all.[8]

In *Assembling California*, the author and amateur geologist John McPhee writes of two disparate timescales – one human and the other geological. According to McPhee, these temporal axes intersect only occasionally,

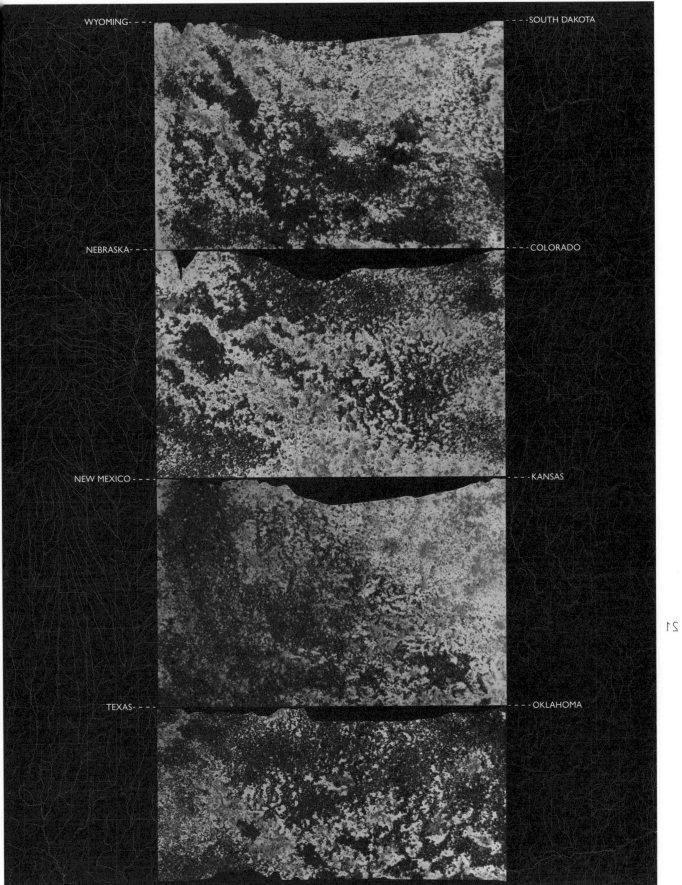

WYOMING - - - -   - - - - SOUTH DAKOTA

NEBRASKA - - -   - - - - COLORADO

NEW MEXICO - - - -   - - - - KANSAS

TEXAS - - - -   - - - - OKLAHOMA

though the effect is often catastrophic.[9]   This junction occurred approximately 70 years ago when human settlement drove a straw into the Ogallala and began to quench its thirst from the water oozing sleepily in the ground.[10]   Prior to this catalytic event, Comanche and Sioux tribes practiced a form of nomadism that utilized natural seeps and springs, and eventually relocated when these ran dry.[11] At this time, the High Plains landscape bore the moniker of "Great American Desert." The region is located within the rain shadow of the Rocky Mountains, and generally exhibits both high rates of evapotranspiration and desiccating winds that wick moisture from its vast and flat landscapes.[12] In certain locations, the aquifer recharges at a rate of less than six millimeters per year.[13]   However, upon discovery of the Ogallala and a seemingly limitless water supply, farmers terraformed the country's most desolate terrain and transformed its economy and global status. By adding water, a bowl of dust became the nation's granary, "breadbasket," and "corn belt."

The High Plains trends towards dust; it is verdant only by virtue of human intervention. The rapid transformation of the mid-west, which was as remarkable as it was untenable, was facilitated by the timely confluence of numerous technological innovations in the Great Plains during the 1940s.[14] Frank Zybach's early center-pivot irrigation system, for instance, utilized boom-mounted water distribution pipes that rotated around a centralized well. This method was ideally suited for the level topography of the High Plains, and the relatively shallow water supply flowing beneath it. Zybach's system slowly generated the circular crop-geometry ubiquitous today across many Mid-western states.[15]   The development of rotary drills with mechanized spinning bits only expedited and increased the efficiency of water mining.[16] As a result, by the 1990s, wells once thought limitless began to run dry, while wells considered marginal were depleted entirely.[17]

Today, an estimated 70% of the Ogallala remains untapped or available for consumption. By 2110, it will have decreased to 13%.[18] The etymology of the word aquifer quite literally translates to *water-bearer or water-bearing*. As a result, aquifers in a human timescale are seen ostensibly as a geologic faucet through which water is delivered to the surface.[19] Yet, our Cartesian surface rationality is fundamentally at odds with the subterranean mystery of this aqueous "stuff".[20] By virtue of its size, heterogeneity, and latency, the Ogallala is less a below ground bathtub than a dynamic geological admixture that muddies the dichotomy between stable earth and liquid morass. Groundwater is an innumerable field of moving rivers entangled intrinsically within earth, not a still pool of water contained by rock. In this way it defies both the linear logic of our relationship with water and the security of our faith in land.

In *Geo-Logic*, the environmental theorist Robert Frodeman suggests that seeing is more than passive visual data collection. Rather it is an active process of filtration and construction, through which symbols are assigned meaning and a spatially oriented narrative is developed. Seeing, in this operational sense, is a fundamental (perhaps the initial) act of design. However, we must also recognize that sight is an individualized and highly personal experience that is accreted slowly through culture, kinesthesia, and subjective comprehension.[21] Representation is a crucial (and ultimately crude) extension of seeing; it is a both method of conveyance and vehicle of translation.

According to Frodeman, true visual intelligence also requires an envisioning of invisible phenomena through which objects are assembled into systems, cycles, and landscapes in an interrogative dream-like collaboration between the mind and the eye.[22] In this conceptual ground, simply because something isn't seen, does not mean it isn't there. To envision groundwater for instance, implies an understanding of its multi-dimensionality and hybridity. It entails a reading and, perhaps more importantly, a willingness to realize the longevity of actions such as contamination and depletion on deep hydrological or geological systems. Representation faces the dual challenge of communicating subjective information, but also of characterizing polyvalent relationships that increasingly and necessarily span temporal and spatial territories.

Certainly, this complexity has been well characterized by landscape architects and theorists including James Corner, Dennis Cosgrove, Anuradha Mathur and Dilip da Cunha, and others who have challenged the Platonic line and reductive notions of Euclidian geometry in landscape representation.[23] In his essay, *Liminal Geometry and Elemental Landscape*, Cosgrove writes that such geometry was used in an act of construction of cultured landscape or urbanism as separate from the "elemental confusion of water and earth".[24] However, most representational approaches to groundwater within the discipline and elsewhere remain mired in Euclid's three foundational elements – points/wells, lines/irrigation networks, and areas/aquifers.

There is undeniably a certain security in this tactic, as it allows us to preserve a degree of ambiguity with respect to water's actual condition. However, this approach imposes a false order upon a fluid milieu for which we lack an imaginative grasp. We see the pipe, not the water it delivers or the resource it diminishes. Such a systematized presentation of the natural world conveys water as an element that is bounded and discrete, not only from ground but also from the settlement that so desperately depends on it.

For landscape architects the tendency to represent natural systems, including groundwater, through conventional modes of architectural drawing is also problematic. According to James Corner, these object-oriented approaches are "precedent to artifice." They present direct analogies to a physical thing with the expectation that it will eventually modify, and ideally improve, a spatial environment.[25] Unfortunately, landscape architects will never build a "solution" to groundwater, nor will they devise a method for reversing almost a century of wanton extraction. While technological innovations will continue to increase the efficiency of our water use, groundwater is slow to forget, and even slower to recharge.

It would be inappropriate to deny the utility of conventional modes of groundwater mapping and modeling. This is a language understood by many and which carries useful information for a range of political, scientific, and analytical purposes. It would also be inadequate to encourage a form of landscape representation that forgoes its criticality and precision in pursuit of a purely artistic rendering. However, if groundwater is simultaneously complicated geology, finite resource, philosophical mystery, and poetic hubris, a visual sensibility predicated upon a binary that suggests something is present, or isn't, will no longer suffice. In our seeing and in our drawing we continue to construct artifactual divides between water and ground, science and poetry, and statistic and provocation. To represent groundwater requires a level of envisioning that accepts the frailty of human effort and the impact of monumental unknowns in the frame of geological timescales.
This is the challenge that faces the landscape architect in his or her agency as designer, scientist, advocate, and artist. We must envision groundwater because of our dependence upon it, and because it is running out; we must represent groundwater to convey why this is so vitally important.

References

1 James A. Miller and Cynthia L. Appel, Groundwater Atlas of the United States, Kansas, Missouri and Nebraska, U.S. Geological Survey HA 730-D, 1997.

2 Wil S. Hylton, "Broken Heartland: The Looming Collapse of Agriculture on the Great Plains," Harper's Magazine, June 2012.

3 V. L. Mcguire, Water-level and Storage Changes in the High Plains Aquifer, Predevelopment to 2011 and 2009—11: U.S. Geological Survey Scientific Investigations Report 2012-5291, 2013. http://pubs.usgs.gov/sir/2012/5291/.

4 Edwin D. Gutengag, Frederick J. Heimes, Noel C. Krothe, Richard R. Luckey, and John B. Weeks. Geohydrology of the High Plains Aquifer in Parts of Colorado, Kansas, Nebraska, New Mexico, Oklahoma, South Dakota, Texas and Wyoming, U.S. Geological Survey Professional Paper 1400-B, 1984.

5 James A. Miller and Cynthia L. Appel, Groundwater Atlas of the United States, Kansas, Missouri and Nebraska, U.S. Geological Survey HA 730-D, 1997.

6 National Park Service statistics, my own calculation.

7 My own calculation.

8 James A. Miller and Cynthia L. Appel, Groundwater Atlas of the United States, Kansas, Missouri and Nebraska, U.S. Geological Survey HA 730-D, 1997.

9 John McPhee, Assembling California (New York: Farrar, Straus and Giroux, 1993).

10 Wil S. Hylton, "Broken Heartland: The Looming Collapse of Agriculture on the Great Plains," Harper's Magazine, June 2012.

11 Wil S. Hylton, "Broken Heartland: The Looming Collapse of Agriculture on the Great Plains," Harper's Magazine, June 2012.

12 Leonard F. Konikow, Groundwater Depletion in the United States (1900-2008): U.S. Geological Survey Scientific Investigations Report 2013-5079. 2013. http://pubs.usgs.gov/sir/2013/5079.

13 Leonard F. Konikow, Groundwater Depletion in the United States (1900-2008): U.S. Geological Survey Scientific Investigations Report 2013-5079. 2013. http://pubs.usgs.gov/sir/2013/5079.

14 Wil S. Hylton, "Broken Heartland: The Looming Collapse of Agriculture on the Great Plains," Harper's Magazine, June 2012.

15 James A. Miller and Cynthia L. Appel, Groundwater Atlas of the United States, Kansas, Missouri and Nebraska, U.S. Geological Survey HA 730-D, 1997.

16 Paul L. Younger, Groundwater in the Environment: An Introduction (Malden, Ma: Blackwell Publishing, 2007).

17 Wil S. Hylton, "Broken Heartland: The Looming Collapse of Agriculture on the Great Plains," Harper's Magazine, June 2012.

18 David R. Steward, Paul J. Bruss, Xiaoying Yang, Scott A. Staggenborg, Stephen Welch, Michael D. Apley, "Tapping Unsustainable Groundwater Stores for Agricultural Production in the High Plains Aquifer of Kansas, Projects to 2110," Proceedings of the National Academy of Science 110, no 37. (2013).

19 Larry L. Mays, Ground and Surface Water Hydrology (Hoboken, New Jersey: John Wiley & Sons, Inc., 2011).

20 Illich, Ivan. H2o and the Waters of Forgetfulness, Reflections on the Historicity of Stuff (Berkeley, CA: Heyday Books, 1985).

21 Corner, James. "Representation and landscape: drawing and making in the landscape medium," Word & Image. Vol. 3. (1992).

22 Frodeman, Robert. Geo-Logic: Breaking Ground Between Philosophy and the Earth Sciences (Albany: State University of New York Press, 2003).

23 Dennis Cosgrove, "Liminal geometry and Elemental Landscape: Construction and Representation." in Recovering Landscape, ed. James Corner (New Jersey: Princeton University Press, 1999) Print.

24 Dennis Cosgrove, "Liminal geometry and Elemental Landscape: Construction and Representation." in Recovering Landscape, ed. James Corner (New Jersey: Princeton University Press, 1999) Print.

25 Corner, James. "Representation and landscape: drawing and making in the landscape medium," Word & Image Vol. 3, (1992).

26

Janet Lee and Kuhn Lee give a fresh look into the processes and politics behind our food system, offering a new perspective to an almost invisible issue.

[consume]

Style Over Substance

Janet Lee + Kuhn Lee

It is a truth universally acknowledged that apocalyptic problems must be in want of a garden. Take, for example, the issue of food security. It began to enter the conversation as a major global concern in the past decade as assumptions about cheap energy, limitless water, and stable climate began to unravel. Over the past 30 years, petroleum—the main source of fuel, fertilizers, and pesticides—has become increasingly scarce and expensive.[1] Water tables are dropping. Aquifers are drying. The climate is becoming more and more unpredictable, and crops are failing from sheer resource exhaustion.[2]

And so Michelle Obama, First Lady of the United States of America, decides to build a garden.

Michelle Obama's kitchen garden at the White House lawn contains 55 different varieties of vegetables including Thomas Jefferson's favorite "tennis ball lettuce".[3] It exemplifies the efforts that are trotted out by numerous designers: small, urban projects with questionable production capabilities. This particular garden is tended by the U.S. Secretary of Agriculture, the White House Horticulturalist, the First Lady herself, and 30 school children from Bancroft Elementary school.[4]

Within a month of the garden being planted, the Mid-America Crop Life Association criticized the Obamas for promoting organic gardening, instead of using chemical fertilizers and other high-yield agricultural techniques.[5] They pointed out that high-yield agriculture is actually better for the environment because it is the only kind of agriculture that allows land conservation and protects global biodiversity.[6] In fact, the third American to ever win the Nobel Peace Prize was Norman Borlaug, who was honored for pioneering the high-yield agricultural practices that saved three continents from starvation and drought in the 1960s.[7]

This begs the question of whether low-yield organic gardening is a plausible food security solution. After all, gardening itself has been a powerful policy tool before. When Thomas Jefferson planted potatoes on the White House lawn he set off a nation-wide trend.[8] And when Eleanor Roosevelt planted a kitchen garden on the White

House lawn during World War II, so many home gardens were started that they produced 40% of all domestic vegetables.[9]

So what does Michelle Obama's garden need to do to successfully address food security?

The Problem

To understand food security, you need to understand one word: surplus. The first time food security existed in human history was around the year 3500 B.C. when we were able to produce the first dependable surplus of food through utilizing the flooding of the Nile.[10] This surplus of food was the first instance that "food security" existed as a concept, and it formed the basis of what we would call civilization.[11] Division of labor was now possible because some human energy could finally be directed away from food procurement. Urbanization was then made possible by a newly created distribution network allowed humans to live away from the site of food production. Social hierarchies took shape over who consumed food, who prepared food, and who produced it. And despite the thousands of years that have passed since, food security and surplus remain inextricably linked as the basic assumptions structuring human civilization.

Food, however, is not biologically suited to be kept at a surplus. To overcome this fact, we proceeded to modify every aspect of the environment and create a web of interdependent solutions. We bred plants to be easier to machine-harvest and transport. We invented a processed-food industry to extend the shelf life of every food source imaginable. We created an international supply chain that allows food to be shipped all over the world.[12] And finally, we have developed the kind of economic system that requires farms to produce more and more every year in order to stay competitive. We have become so "successful" at negotiating the gap between biology and economy through this cycle of surplus, distribution and consumption that if we stick to our current pattern of production and consumption, we will now need to produce more food over the next 40 years than we have ever had to produce in the past 8,000 years combined.[13]

To solve this issue at the regional scale would require social and economic cooperation well beyond the scope of landscape architecture. And to solve this issue at the global scale would require an unprecedented degree of political action and collaboration, not to mention the deployment of new technologies. These political, economic and technological solutions are neither our forté nor under our purview as landscape architects and designers. And yet, if surplus food is the problem, then the answer to food security is actually pretty simple: produce less, eat less, waste less. We can no longer propose solutions that leave our production and consumption habits unchanged.

More importantly, we can no longer propose solutions that do not ask for radical changes in behavior. Although this is the point of every political, economic and logical measure, most of these so-called solutions fail because they lack community support. Thus, instead of trying to design the solution, what if we shift our thinking towards enabling the solution? Can we reframe the question by asking how we can make the necessary lifestyle changes emotionally acceptable through design?

Enabling the Solution

Another political garden built during a previous food security crisis offers an insight into what this might mean for designers. This garden was built in 1774, when Prussia was on the verge of a famine after years of war had ravaged the countryside. King Frederick the Great decided that cultivation of a new vegetable called a potato as a secondary crop would bring stability and protection against famine. It seemed the ultimate silver-bullet solution: not only did potatoes provide almost all essential nutrients, but they were easy to grow and harvest.[14] Unfortunately, despite royal edicts and death threats, the Prussian peasantry refused to comply. They looked upon the potato with a mixture of disgust and fear. They were further supported by the clerics who accused potato plants of being both unbiblical and an aphrodisiac.[15] The lack of cultural acceptance made the potato a dead end – until Frederick switched tactics.

He named the potato "a royal crop" fit only for a king. He installed a fence around the garden, and he stationed soldiers around the "royal field" to guard it day or night. Most importantly, he gave the guards secret instructions to not guard the field very carefully at night. This enabled the curious peasantry to sneak into the field at night to steal potatoes and have an opportunity to try this scandalous new dish. It was thus that the potato swiftly made its way into the Prussian diet and became responsible for the next wave of food security in Europe that lasted until the onset of World War I.[16]

If we return to the original question of Michelle Obama's garden with the Prussian example in mind, we can start to understand how designers can regain agency in the face of such an overwhelmingly complex global issue. On the surface the gardening efforts are fairly similar. After all, both are small interventions that function as a top-down approach to inspire bottom-up policy changes. Both gardens are attempts to reframe the conversation. And both are working with symbolic solutions on a national stage. Their approaches, however, contain two critical differences.

First, Frederick's garden appealed to desire as the driver of change, whereas the Obama garden appealed to morality. While morality can be a strong force, it has a very short shelf life when it is not enforced by policy. Eleanor Roosevelt's "victory garden" campaign had inspired 5 million vegetable gardens, but as soon as the food rationing and government propaganda stopped, the gardens quickly and quietly disappeared. All told, mass public gardening had only been able to sustain itself in America for three years. In contrast, Frederick's solution took on a life of its own because it was introduced through desire. Instead of prescribing a single action, Frederick inspired a thousand permutations, recipes, and uses that were desired and accepted. To this day, visitors still leave potatoes as a mark of respect on the grave of Frederick the Great. Not only are potatoes still planted, but they are considered the fifth most important crop in the world.[17]

30 This leads to the second important difference. Obama's organic backyard garden attempts to function outside of the surplus framework. Although organic home gardening could solve aspects of distribution and consumption, the economics of a solution based on volunteer labor and small, inefficient scales of production do not make sense within the current surplus framework. The production capability for the three most important staples of the urban diet — corn, milk and beef — is murky at best. Frederick's solution, on the other hand, was to reframe the conversation within the framework of surplus: production, distribution, and consumption. Introducing the potato was a sensible solution that addressed all three components of food security by bringing down costs and raising the surplus,. Bbut it is also a solution that cannot work in today's world of rapidly shrinking resources. As the fertilizer lobbyists pointed out, the most disturbing part of the Obama garden may be that it proposes a solution to food security that is not based on creating a surplus at all.

Reimagining Ideals

It is an interesting question asked at an interesting time. Can food security exist without a surplus?

The past decades have been marked by the discovery that the various assumptions we have based our food system on are crumbling. In addition to assumptions about bottomless resources, the assumption about the relationship between information and power is also changing; as information is no longer scarce, but the ability to make sense of it is. Even the assumption of price is starting to crack, as cheaper and bigger is no longer better. In this newly forming paradigm of food security, the fastest growing sector of the food economy is expensive organic produce and the most powerful driver is no longer price, but narrative and desire.

One of the key indicators of this changing food landscape is the supermarket pastoral phenomenon. Coined by journalist Michael Pollan, supermarket pastoral refers to the genre of elaborate and rapidly proliferating pastoral images and narratives used to attract attention to organic products. According to economist Richard Lanham, "attracting attention is what style is all about" and in an aisle full of cheaper choices, these labels have the power to evoke desire and change consumer behavior. In fact, Pollan argues that "one of the key innovations of organic food was to allow some more information to pass along the food chain between producer and consumer." Using landscape as a medium, the organic food industry has successfully created an $11 billion industry based on desire.[18]

At the same time, however, the industry is trapped in an obsolete framework bounded by supermarket pastoral that does not allow it to truly grapple with current realities of resource depletion. As soon as landscape was adopted as the narrative medium, the industry and general public could only see it as part of a stylized pastoral tradition promoting an anti-urban, deeply nostalgic, and very romantic form of un-mechanized nature. These deeply rooted associations make it difficult for urban areas to have truly "local" farms, since "nature" should be nostalgic and far away from cities. And the idea of un-mechanized nature actually makes high-quality food more scarce and expensive, rather than less. Instead of adding up to a more sustainable system, these components have been combined in a way that makes it impossible to achieve wide-spread change.

The organic food movement started out with a premise based on locally-sourced, higher-quality produce, and a more sustainable way of life. These ideas have been quickly usurped by cheap clichés of rolling pastures, happy cows, and whimsical vegetables. The dichotomy within the landscape images of supermarket pastoral shows that style has misshapen the substance of the organic movement. And it is our fault that there is no other ideal to replace the pastoral. Despite their best efforts, neither Michelle Obama nor the organic industry can accomplish this without our help.

Lanham was right to argue that attracting attention is what style is all about.[19] But merely attracting attention does not make a difference until it changes behavior. Rather than just attracting attention, we need to guide it to enable solutions. And as shown by the organic food movement, it is only through using the right style that we will be able to get to the right substance. Thus if food security could be understood in one word, perhaps the solution could best be understood in three: Style over Substance.

References

1 Roberts, Paul, The End of Food (New York: Houghton Mifflin, 2008), 12.

2 Roberts, Paul, The End of Food, 12

3 Black, Jane "The First Garden Gets Its First Planting". The Washington Post. March 6, 2010.

4 Burros, Marian "Obamas to Plant Vegetable Garden at White House". The New York Times. (March 19, 2009).

5 Naughton, Philippe "Big Agriculture takes Umbrage at Mrs Obamas Organic Garden". The Times (London). (April 22, 2009).

6 Angelsen, A., and Kaimowitz, D. 2001. "The Role of Agricultural Technologies in Tropical Deforestation." Agricultural Technologies and Tropical Deforestation. CABI Publishing, New York

7 Stuertz, Mark. "Green Giant." Dallas Observer. (December 5, 2002).

8 Higgins, Adrian "Jefferson the Gardener Set His Sights High to Reap the Earth's Bounty". The Washington Post. (April 5, 2009).

9 Woolley, John T.; Peters, Gerhard. "Franklin D. Roosevelt: Statement Encouraging Victory Gardens". The American Presidency Project. University of California, Santa Barbara.

10 Roberts, Paul, The End of Food, 11.

11 Kiple, Kenneth and Ornelas, Kriemhild, eds., The Cambridge World History of Food, vol. 2 (Cambridge: Cambridge University Press, 2000), 1126.

12 Roberts, Paul, The End of Food, xiv-xvii.

13 Peirce, Neil, "Cities and Food: Quandary, Opportunity." Citiwire, March 23, 2013 http://citiwire.net/columns/cities-and-food-quandary-opportunity/

14 "International Year of the Potato 2008 – The Potato". United Nations Food and Agricultural Organisation. 2009.

15 Mann, Charles C., "How the Potato Changed the World," Smithsonian Magazine, (November 2011).

16 Neil, William H., "What if Pizarro Had Not Found Potatoes in Peru?" in What If? eds. Bradley, J. and Cowley, R., (New York: Penguin Putnam Inc. 2002), 413.

17 "International Potato Center," http://cipotato.org/potato/facts.

18 Pollan, Michael. The Omnivore's Dilemma. New York: The Penguin Press, 2006.

19 Lanham, Richard. The Economics of Attention: Style and Substance in the Age of Information. (Chicago: Chicago University Press. 2006)

Using Waste as the substance of investigation, Alyssa Olson envisages an imaginative spectacle that resides in all of our psyches but actually materializing in the Pacific Ocean, the 8th continent: Away.

[waste]

Away

Alyssa Olson

As a phenomenon exacerbated by the Anthropocene era, waste is produced by two basic elements: material mass and human consumption over time. Consumption inevitably results in waste accumulation across myriad landscapes. Abiding by no law other than gravity, waste morphs as an ephemeral creature hugging the earth. A viral, synthetic pox capable of suffocating, enlivening and territorializing ecosystems, waste is here to stay and grow with the human population.

The destiny of waste is a utilitarian spectacle. Away is the eighth continent. Located on the edge of nowhere, Away is the most common place on earth. First conceived in the 14th century by the French[1], the notion of waste proliferated in the late 19th century due to overwhelming social awareness of "health, aesthetics, affluence, technology and quality of urban life."[2] With no role to fill, waste was forced to go Away. Embracing its role as an invisible passenger aboard terrestrial and hydrological modes of transport en route its destination, this rogue creature loiters about until its use-by date. Robots are venturing Away to reunite with old friends.

In the untended grounds of Away, the mind never dwells but the body may do so. Jardim Gramacho, on the periphery of Rio de Janeiro, is one of the world's self-proclaimed largest garbage dumps.[3] Landfill pickers—Catadores—thrive here. Like ants atop their nest, they sift valuables and repurpose them as jewelry and furniture.[4]

Unlike uninhabited landfills, Jardim Gramacho is a diamond in the rough. Uninhabited landfills are dead landscapes. Typical refuse spaces lie fallow unless a designer plays 'God' to 'fix' them. Programmed parks are but corsets, choking buried truths beneath wafting perfumes of methane and stale air.

Waste is a significant recorder of human existence. Its memories are of human obsessions with economy. Trails waste leaves behind contradict an illusory image of a species capable of controlling environments. The notion of lifestyle is Homo sapiens' anticipation of survival coupled with comfort. Away broadcasts how the earth mirrors life patterns. Deconstructed, this great feat of archaeological espionage reveals humanity's Pandora's box. A messy whole inferior to the sum of its pristine parts, Away is transforming before our wide-shut eyes from its compartmentalized locale in the collective human mind to become the largest construct on earth.

Design objects, predecessors to the castaway-heathens populating Away, are mutants bred with aloof intent. The organization of their aqueous amalgamation is similar to roots of mangroves continually seeking new space to grow. Every consumer is a builder of this Tower of Babel whose genesis is in each hypothalamus. Away engenders the mental map of Homo sapiens' existence. It unveils human symbiosis with waste and deluges of memories reigning upon it.

Like Jardim Gramacho, Away is sustained by a cannibalistic scavenger diet. Recycling as an industry is no longer a threat to landfill starvation, so nomadic archaeologists like those at Gramacho may hunt and gather objects abound. Transformative topographies capture human progress throughout time. Away is a silent index impregnated by invisible forces. A Cesarean section through it at once ignites nostrils and unmutes silenced objects. This machine-made landscape is capable of sparking economies and lifestyles, just as the Catadores experience each day.

In a world of seven billion humans aspiring to 10 or 11 billion by 2100,[5] future human habitats will inevitably increase in density. These inflated hubs are not without increased waste streams. Terrestrial marginalization of this renewable dissipates as humans need living space. Away gains superiority through aqueous waste abundance at the mouth of every stream.

A covert operation, Away remains an ambiguous murmuration of brooding otherness. Away currently crawls in infancy as an infamous plastic soup stewing across the Pacific. Commonly referred to as the trash vortex, Earth's United States of Waste is bounded by mass consumption and a plenitude of abandoned materials. Strewn across torrent seas into the depths of the ocean and back, the hostile human relationship with Away remains intact despite its ill nature.

Brewing in the back of minds, the instant gratification of Away is a trap. Saying its name inserts this non-place into reality then switches one's mind into a combinatory mode of forgiving and forgetting. Like a familiar back-country destination, the seduction of this vacuum is mentioned by happenstance but understood as an unworldly, resilient place. Strikingly similar is the connection fortunate children have with a first stuffed animal, which is an on-demand presence to satisfy a need for comfort. Human satisfaction is programmed into the lost-and-found gardens of Away.

Trapped between a blanket of ultraviolet rays and cool washes of plankton, a wrinkling mass floats atop a salty liquid of innumerable livelihoods. Recharged with layered crusts of human residue, its most tired layers slowly drown in a trench more than seven miles below daylight. Ripened by time and dark secrets Away goes with the flows of currents and tides. Human-driven currents cycle clockwise by the day while tides whirl clockwise about the Pacific around its sub-tropical gyre.[6] Together they stir the saucy cesspool. At this scale discharged naval ropes are merely noodles tussling about oily mystery meats and seasonal sauce blends.

Happily congealing as a Pacific stew, Away is the most intelligent of all pink elephants. Its every aspect is designed. Evolved in convergence, its stylish organs have been evaluated under microscopes, scrutinized by economic climates and adopted throughout time. Conceived within a shifting constellation of human ingenuity, the same brains responsible for creating Away cast it 'away'. This bipolar stance affirms humans conceive their territory in terms of what exists within and without. Away is optimally suited for conditions unfit for human life. Unpredictable saltwater fluxes, extreme ultraviolet exposure and unfathomed environmental conditions are endured at Away as humans are not programmed to manage these conditions.

Arisen out of the blue this continent feeds off international industries. Economies of manufacturing produce maximal quantities of products in timely cycles. Waste within these cycles are free lunches for Away though they come at great costs to earth's resources. The evolution of this continent will occur at a faster rate as technological feats breed more invasive synthetic materials. The materiality of Away gains strength through new successional product generations. A common product species is the Plastic bottle.

The most popular manufactured species holds captive one of the world's most precious resources: water. Plastic bottles are indirect descendants of human hands. These liquid-holding formations store and transfer water with intent of sustaining human life. Habitat, lifespan and genetic inheritances limit natural species while manufactured species are exempt. Bred in production environments, new product species are manufactured and evolve with cycles of economy and ideas through synthetic selection. Plastic bottles have derived through synthetic selection and enable new forms of competition with other manufactured species.

Glass bottles are endangered within plastic novelty ecosystems. By altering the financial climates of two liquid assets driving humanity, money and water, this invasive slowly asphyxiates its competition.

These synthetic nuggets evolve with human society yet proliferate in 24-hour cycles. Similar to beak variations in Darwin's Galapagos finches, Plastic bottles have adapted to environments of convenience: travel, home refrigeration, retail and so on. Bottles vary by material genus including high and low density polyethylene, polyethylene terephtalate, polyvinyl chloride, polypropylene, polystyrene and fluorine treated.[7] Each genus is programmed for different environmental conditions and contributes to species diversity at Away.

Of the 200 billion pounds of plastic produced in the world every year, a guesstimated 30 parts per million end up on the ocean floor.[8] Underwater stalagmites link foundations of Away to its floating stalactite counterpart. The United Nations Environment Programme (UNEP) estimated there are 46,000 pieces of floating plastic per square mile in the alpha male soup. Sentenced to an environment in perpetual flux, these plastic bits are discovering the depths of the ocean faster than humans.

Away is growing at an accelerating pace. Produced at increasingly faster rates manufactured species are facing challenges of population growth. Placed into the Pacific in 130-million-pound increments[9] these young species are manufactured to last longer than predecessor species. The hemorrhage of undesired products penetrates deep into the future as a lackadaisical utopia.

Away embodies this human desire. Away is here.

References

1 Douglas Harper, Online Etymology Dictionary, 2013, accessed September 02, 2013. http://www.etymonline.com/

2 Mira Engler, "Waste Landscapes: Permissable Metaphors in Landscape Architecture," Landscape Journal, Volume 15, Issue 1, Spring 1995. 11-25.

3 Marilia Brocchetto and Azadeh Ansari, Landfill's closure changing lives in Rio, CNN, 05 June 2012, Accessed August 30, 2013. http://www.cnn.com/2012/06/05/world/americas/brazil-landfill-closure/index.html

4 Ibid.

5 Molly McElroy, "UW research: World Population Could Be Nearly 11 Billion by 2100," University of Washington, Seattle, Washington, 13 June 2013, accessed August 30, 2012. http://www.washington.edu/news/2013/06/13/uw-research-world-population-could-be-nearly-11-billion-by-2100/

6 Alison Cawood "Coriolis Force and Convergence Zones" in Seaplex: Seeking the Science of the Garbage Patch, 04 August 2009, accessed August 30, 2013. http://seaplexscience.com/2009/08/04/coriolis-force-and-convergence-zones/

7 "The 7 Most Common Plastics and How They are Typically Used," Reuseit: Reusables for Every Part of Your Life, 2013, accessed August 18, 2013. http://www.reuseit.com/product-materials/the-7-most-common-plastics-and-how-they-are-typically-used.htm

8 Michelle Allsopp et al, Plastic Debris in the World's Oceans, UN Environment Program, Greenpeace International, June 2006. 1-43.

9 Ibid.

Challenging the connotation of the term 'urbanism', Youngsoo Kim provides insight into Chengdu's emergent and generic nature.

[grow]

The Generic Garden
Youngsoo Kim

While global population reached seven billion in 2010, its growth rate has been declining from 2.2 percent to 1.1 percent for the last four decades. During the same period, global urban population growth has been exploding with a 168 percent total increase and a 2.41 percent annual growth rate occurring mostly in the developing world.[1] Although urban models vary from place to place, the global phenomenon of rapid urbanization in the context of a globalized economy has been met predominantly by what Rem Koolhaas called the "Generic City". Koolhaas sees the Generic City's "lack of uniqueness as a virtue, absence is a vacuum always needing to be filled, reworked, redefined. In generic cities, buildings become floating signifiers, divorced from programmatic content and historical past...they are pragmatic and able to change to fit new needs...like a Hollywood studio lot, generic city can produce a new identity every Monday morning"[2]. While architecture seeks new potential in the generic, no such possibility is afforded to landscape. The landscape is expected to anchor the global city in place and landscape architects generally go to great lengths to ensure that this is the case. In this paper I ask whether landscape architecture can exploit the conditions of generic urbanism to generate a new landscape of emerging cities in the developing world. To explore this question we visit the city of Chengdu, the engine of the Chinese government's "Go West" initiatives.

A city of over 14 million people, Chengdu is a hotbed of investment in inland China and, at least according to Mundell and Yi, a leader in new approaches to urbanization.[3] Possibly inspired by Lee Kuan Yew's success in Singapore, in 2009 with growing environmental and social awareness, the city of Chengdu adopted the slogan of "Garden City" in search of an overarching theme that both fulfills the demands for industrialization, modernization, and urbanization, and ameliorates problems such as pollution, congestion, urban-rural disparity, and the loss of fertile farmland. After hosting the Architecture Biennale in 2011 and the Garden City Forum in 2012, Chengdu expressed its ambition to be the largest 'garden city' in the world.[4]

The Garden City concept was advanced by Ebenezer Howard in 1902 for a population of 32,000 people fusing the best of town and country.[5] Intended as an agrarian antidote to industrialization, Howard's Garden City ended up becoming car-fueled 20th century suburbia. How then does this idea of the Garden City translate to a city of 14 million in Western China and what role might landscape architecture play in that unlikely translation?

Ever since Deng Xiaoping's declaration of economic reform in 1978 (and with his open admiration for Singapore), Chinese cities have been looking for urbanization 'with Chinese characteristics'. The megacities that experienced explosive growth after being designated as Special Economic Zones, such as Shanghai and Shenzhen, generated neither a model with distinctive Chinese attributes, nor a model that balances economic growth and environmental protection. Kate Orff argues that the 'garden city' in China is "a centralized idea, a unifying, apolitical, and upbeat slogan that is sufficiently vague to allow the most ambitious proposals to appear virtuous."[6]

In this case, the Garden City works to conceal the brutality and homogeneity of rapid urbanization.

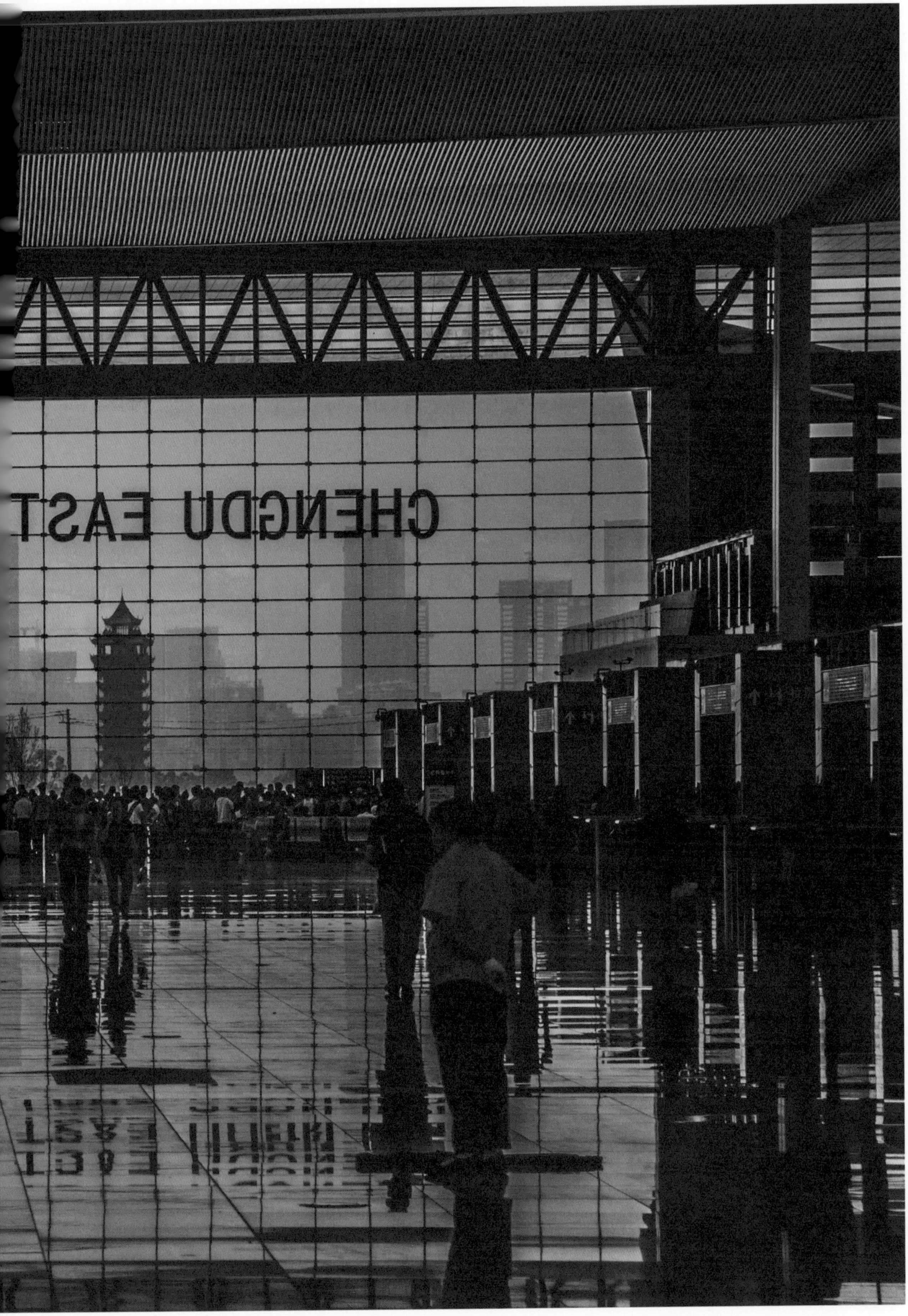
CHENGDU EAST

In Chengdu, Tianfu Software Park, a project in the midst of the city's most ambitious and heavily promoted 'Tianfu New Area,' exemplifies the propaganda of the Garden City. The 'Park' aims to build a self contained city for 40,000 employees of global companies within the city.[7] Pristine high-rise buildings, regardless of their purpose, are situated in the middle of amorphous green space and massive tree-lined boulevards isolate the development from the city beyond. Another sub-project of Tianfu New Area includes iconic buildings such as the New Century Global Building, (the world's biggest single-structure building), and Zaha Hadid's Contemporary Art Center, currently under construction. These overblown 'signifiers' float in a sea of paved surfaces.

The Garden City of Chengdu is a masked machine of generic landscape delivered by centralized, top-down master planning and profit-seeking developers. This chemistry of formal planning and swift execution is the essence of the generic city. For its critics the Generic City is a social and environmental disaster in the making. According to the architectural critic Edward Denison, there are few architects in China who challenge or strategically maneuver around the prevailing planning framework.[8] Steven Holl and developer CapitaLand are exceptions. In Raffles City, Chengdu, Holl worked at a human scale to provide the (SoHo – small office/home office) urbanity an emerging urban class of young professionals and entrepreneurs desire.[9] In a similar vein, projects that retrofit urban fragments in-between the surge of the generic city are increasingly evident. Resembling the 798 art-district project in Beijing, which repurposes existing industrial buildings into art space funded by domestic and foreign galleries, there is the Eastern Suburbs Memory project in Chengdu, which reuses an electronic manufacturing facility as a musical performance and production venue for artists on the eastern fringe of the city. By virtue of their difference to the system of the Generic City, these places succeed as cultural hotspots for a certain social group but they never seriously undermine the modus operandi of the Generic City.

While difference is finding its way into the generic in regards to urban design in China, landscape architecture is yet to create something other than the Garden City. Landscape architecture serves as an apology for the Generic City. Landscape architecture places mere band-aids over its deep social and ecological wounds.

There is an opportunity for landscape architecture to play a leading role by making use of the Generic City's dynamism to generate a new landscape of the city. Landscape architecture can contribute to shaping an emerging new landscape that moves beyond the generic toward unprecedented and creative new urban models. When it is expecting another 400 million people in the next fifteen years in urban China, cities like Chengdu, undergoing explosive transformation, can be a testing ground for novel approaches. Landscape architecture in China should be critical of its deployment as cosmetic surgery for the Generic City and work towards revealing its contradictions.

References

1 United Nations Department of Economic and Social Affairs, Population Division (2013). World Population Prospects: The 2012 Revision (New York: United Nations 2013).

2 Rem Koolhaas, "Generic City", S,M,L,XL, (New York: Monacelli Press, 1995) 1249-1250.

3 Robert A. Mundell and Li Yining, "The Way to Urbanization during Go-west Campaign: a Case Study on Chengdu" (Beijing: China State Information Center, 2010). See also, Chengdu Statistic Yearbook (Chengdu, 2012).

4 Lucy Bulliant, "Chengdu, China: Big city symbiosis," Urbanista 1 (2013), http://www.urbanista.org/issues/issue-1/features/chengdu-big-city-symbiosis.

5 Ebenezer Howard, "Garden cities of tomorrow", (London: S. Sonnenschein & Co., Ltd., 1902).

6 Kate Orff, "Landscape, Zhuhai" in Chuihua J Chung, et al.,The Great Leap Forward: Harvard Design School project of the city, (Cologne: Tashen, 2001), 364.

7 "Tianfu New Area: 'New Engine' for Western Economic Growth," http://www.sc.gov.cn/10462/10758/10760/10766/2012/5/2/102 08506.shtml.

8 Edward Denison, "China's macro-planning policies: Architectural catalyst or constraint?" Architecture Design 82 No. 5 (2012), 54.

9 Michiel Hulshof and Daan Roggenveen, "Heaven for young leaders who enjoy life and shopping," in China's New Megacities: How the city moved to Mr. Sun (Amsterdam: SUN, 2011), 108–131.

The Keystone XL pipeline offers a newfound relationship between landscape architecture and infrastructure. Michael Ockrant Shafir uncovers it through the ubiquitous nature of oil.

[unearth]

This Is Not A Pipe
Michael Ockrant Shafir

The Keystone XL Pipeline (KXL) is a proposed addition and extension to the existing Keystone Pipeline that has been commissioned by the TransCanada Corporation. Along with one existing and two other proposed pipelines, the KXL Network will form a fossil fuel vein that is planned to bifurcate the North American continent from Hardisty in the north, to Houston in the south. For some a life-line to energy independence, for others a monument to climate change denial, the KXL network is the biggest landscape project currently being undertaken in North America.

At depths of thousands of meters below the ground, fossil fuels are natural energies formed in the geologic past from the remains of living organisms that lived over five hundred million years ago. Sectionally suspended through numerous strata of earth, fossil fuels exist in ranges of deposits that span the entire surface of the globe, permeating both aqueous and terrestrial terrain. Diverse in ranges of quantity and composition, reserves vary from steaming hot liquids in far-away deserts, to semi-solid deposits in northern territories, such as the reserves in Hardisty, Alberta.

The KXL vein will begin in Hardisty's tar sands–a bituminous admixture of sand, clay and water spanning over 350,000 square kilometers of boreal forests and peat bogs.[1] As such, the Athabasca tar sands represent a globally significant reserve of crude oil. Unlike conventional methods of extraction, the unrefined, viscous oil suspended in these sands requires the use of a variety of novel extraction techniques because of its consistency and varying location within the ground. Temporarily suspending functioning ecological systems, the extraction process sets up technologic and economic modes of operation within the landscape, thus giving birth to the KXL.

In contrast to the glaringly visible processes of extraction, the crude oil is planned to travel to its destination incognito. Swallowing a projected 1.8 million barrels of diluted bitumen per day, the crude oil is planned to travel through its shiny steel casing of 91.4 centimeters in diameter and 5.24 centimeters in material thickness.[2] Slithering its way anonymously through the landscape of Alberta (while continually being added to along the way), through the rugged landscapes of Montana, South Dakota, Nebraska, Kansas, and Oklahoma, the KXL's trajectory will end in Texas.[3] Depending on the landscape, the pipeline will run over, along or under the surface of the earth. Although the risks associated with its trajectory are claimed to be minimal, there are undeniable risks when puncturing sensitive terrain, such as the Ogallala aquifer, which supplies freshwater for about two million people.[4]

Once the crude oil reaches its destination in Texas, would be refined through a process of separation and evaporation, molecular cracking and rearranging, and chemical balancing.[5] From there, the oil would be ready for shipment and consumption around North America and the world.

The KXL prompts two important, interdependent conversations to be had in relationship to the discipline of landscape architecture, both of which conclude that the discipline must be willing to contribute to, and learn from the opportunities that the KXL brings forward.

First, the KXL offers the dual possibility of broadening the scope of built projects for the profession as well as humanizing the physicality of the oil vein. Fifty years ago, the conversation around a pipeline would not have entered the disciplinary realm of landscape architecture. Not anymore. Today, the various sites, stations and veins that make up the migrations of fossil fuel here and around the world have indeed become part of the conversation within the discipline. From Duisburg Nord and the re-interpretation of industrial grounds, to Freshkills Park and the re-imagining of a landfill, contemporary landscape architecture's built scope and ambition has evolved and broadened its horizons beyond the pastoral to the post-industrial and infrastructural. In so doing, the discipline has started to cultivate an ever-widening portfolio of built, post-industrial works.[6] However, it is important to note the lack of evidence to suggest that a single landscape architect has actively participated on the design or conception of a real pipeline project anywhere in the world.[7] This is partly due to the lack of interest on the commissioning and engineering side, but also from the design side as well. But, as the increasing demand for resources pushes us to extract from vulnerable territories and subsequently transport through sensitive and populated areas, the need for landscape architecture to be present across all phases of oil operations as part of the groundwork for conceiving pipelines becomes increasingly relevant and necessary. Landscape architecture should thus be the structuring agent upon which pipelines (and their resulting grounds of operation) interact with cities, communities, neighborhoods, and of course, the environment.

Second, as the KXL represents an infrastructure project that landscape architects should be involved with in a real sense, modernity has rendered the origin and endpoint of resources invisible to the consumer which I believe has revealed acute aesthetic and ethical challenges in terms of the relationship between design agency and oil pipelines.

A pipeline represents and solidifies a dichotomous connection between life and land, energy and earth, which is neither an accurate nor healthy understanding of our relationship to the planet. The evolution of the human understanding of resources can be traced through its etymology. The word resource as we understand it today came from the Latin word surgere which meant 'to rise' but later evolved into the Old French word resourdre, which meant 'to recover'.[8] The former definition frames a conception of a resource as something that originates from the land, whereas the latter situates a resource as something that has been discovered and can thus be owned. The repercussions of the latter part of this pivotal shift have been reinforced throughout history. As Lewis Mumford noted in respect of Henry George's sarcastic observation that, "the physiocrat's notion that all wealth comes ultimately from the land – and whoever denies this denies the solar and chemical and organic basis of life", one can see that the pipeline is still to this day very much an historic phenomenon cloaked in contemporary material.[9] Engraining the division between life and land and rendering this physical, the pipeline further objectifies oil by removing it from the complex system from which it originates and invisibly delivers it to its user. We do the same with our water, our electricity, and our food because modernity has told us this must be so.

In his theory of consumption, Karl Marx argued that consumption operates as a seamless machine when divorced from production.[10] When the worlds of extraction, transportation and refinement are left behind, hidden and forgotten in far-away places, the commodity floats around in an innocent, invisible and unecological way, divorced from the physical and environmental consequences of its existence. The commodity of oil in particular adds two layers of complexity to its existence. First, its trajectory from refinement to light bulb follows global networks of transportation and production that have visibly negative, physical impacts on the landscape. Second, beyond transportation and production, oil finds its way into our lives through an infinite number of objects, processes and food products to the point that one is no longer conscious of its omnipresence. On one hand, the sheer physicality of the extraction and refinement

paired with the embedded presence of oil in everyday life, and on the other, the necessity for broadened forms of engagement from landscape architects.

Because landscape architects communicate primarily through physical space, the KXL pipeline brings the opportunity and necessity to expand the architectural languages through which we operate in order to enter and practice as designers in the extensive world of the petrochemical lifecycle. In addition to design languages of the picturesque and the sublime, broadening our design vocabulary to encompass techniques of rendering visible the physical and ecological implications of petrochemical commodities suggest a crucial aspect to the future relevance of the discipline in regards to energy consumption and resource depletion. In this regard, the KXL offers landscape architects an opportunity to practice beyond oil operations on the ground to a further-reaching project that spatializes and makes apparent the ramifications of the pipeline's use, operation, and consumption to the people who will consume the KXL's energy and products every day. This would sever the dichotomous relationship between life and land, earth and energy by forging a relationship between design agency and oil pipelines.

Hence, the KXL is a phenomenon that landscape architects can explore with regard to not only its immediate incursions in to the landscape but the entire system of production and consumption from which it stems. As Kate Orff argues in 'Petrochemical America', landscape architects have a capacity to holistically communicate the social, economic and environmental issues embodied in major infrastructural developments.[11]

As such, landscape architecture should give expression to its role as a mediator between production and consumption. Not only can we assist in designing the way the pipeline occupies the landscape along its extensive route, but we can also conceive of long-term futures for such a system. For example, the pipeline could become a multi-functional, bundled infrastructural system that transports crude oil, facilitates a high-speed train, and hosts a migratory pathway for animals making their way south. As crude oil is phased out of production, the pipeline could act as a repository for rainwater collection, a modern aqueduct, bringing millions of gallons of water to farms that are currently in desperate need of reliable

Husky Prince Refinery 10 800
Shell Scotford Refinery 100 000
IMPERIAL OIL STRATHCONA REFINERY 195 000
PETRO CANADA EDMONTON REFINERY 135 000
HUSKY LLOYDINSTER REFINERY 25 000
CONCO PHILIPS FERNDALE REFINERY 96 000
TESORO ANACORTES REFINERY 108 000
SHELL ANACORTES REFINER 145 000
US OIL AND REFINING TACOMA 35 000
MONTANA REFINING COMPANY REFINERY 8 200
TESORO MANDAN REFINERY 58 000
Flint Hills LP Saint Paul Refinery 265 000
Petro Canada Montreal Refinery 130 000
Ultramar (Valero) Jean-Gaulin Refinery
Irving Oil Limited Refinery 250 000
Imperial Oil Dartmouth Refinery 89 000
North Atlantic Refining Come by Chance Refinery 105 000
Cenex Harvest States Coop Refinery 55 000
ConcoPhilips Billings Refinery 58 000
ExxonMobil Billings Refinery 60 000
Wyoming Refining Co, Newcastle Refinery 12 500
Tesoro West Coast, Salt Lake Refinery 58 000
Sinclair Oil, Sinclair Refinery 66 000
Little America Refining Co, Evensville Refinery 24 500
Frontier Refining Inc, Cheyenne Refinery 46 000
Colorado Refining Co, Commerce City Refinery 27 000
NCRA McPherson Refinery 81 200
Frontier Refining and Marketing Inc, El Dorado Refinery 103 000
ConocoPhilips Wood River Refinery 306 000
Coffeyville Resources Refinery 112 000
ConocoPhilips, Ponca City Refinery 194 000
Sunoco Inc, Tulsa Refinery 83 200
Marathon Ashland Petroleum LLC, Robinson Refinery 192 000
Countrymark Cooperative Inc, Mount Vernon Refinery 23 000
Marathon Ashland Petroleum LLC, Canton Refinery 73 000
Kern Oil and Refining Company, Bakersfield Refinery 25 000
ExxonMobil, Joilet Refinery 238 000
Bp, Whiting Refinery 410 000
PDV Midwest Refining LLC, Lemont Refinery 160 000
Premcor Refining Group Inc, Lima Refinery 158 400
Imperial Oil, Nanticoke Refinery 65 000
Bp, Toledo Refinery 160 000
Marathon Ashland Petroleum LLC, Detroit Refinery 74 000
Premcore Refining Group Inc, Delaware Refinery 175 000
ConocoPhilips, Trainer Refinery 185 000
Sunoco, Marcus Hook Refinery 175 000
Valero Refining Co, Paulsberg Refinery 160 000
Citgo, Paulsboro Refinery 51 000
Sunoco, Westville Refinery 145 000
Chevron Inc USA 80 000
ConocoPhilips, Linden Refinery 230 000
Chevron, Richmond Refinery 243
Shell Oil, Martinez Refinery 155 000
Giant Yorktown Refinery 58 600
Ergon West Virginia Inc Refinery 19 400
ConocoPhilips, Santa Maria Refinery 42 000
Chevron, El Segundo Refinery 260 000
Exxon Mobil Torrance Refinery 149 000
BP, West Coast Products Refinery 260 000
ConocoPhilips, Wilmington Refinery 133 000
Paramount Petroleum Corporation Refinery 54 000
Edgington Oil Compant, Long Beach Refinery 26 000
ConocoPhilips Santa Maria Refinery 42 000
Giant Industries Inc, Bloomsfield Refinery 16 800
Giant Industries Inc, Ciniza Gallup Refinery 26 000
ConocoPhilips Borger Refinery 146 000
Valero Energy Corp Sunray Refinery 175 000
Wynnewood Refining Co Refinery 52 000
TPI Petro Inc Ardmore Refinery 74 400
La Gloria Oil and Gas Co Refinery 55 000
Lion Oil Company, El Dorado Refinery 70 000
Ergon Refining Inc, Vicksburg Refinery 23 000
Hunt Refining Co, Tuscaloosa Refinery 33 500
Citgo Savannah Refinery, 28 000
Navajo Refining Co, Artesia Refinery 75 000
Alon USA LP, Big Spring Refinery 61 000
Citgo Corpus, Christi Refinery 156 000
ConocoPhilips, Sweeny Refinery 229 000
BP, Texas City Refinery 437 000
Lyondell Citgo Refining, Houton Refinery 270 200
Deer Park Refining LTD Partnership Refinery 333 700
ExxonMobil Baytown Refinery 557 000
Motiva Enterprises LLC, Port Arthur Refinery 285 000
Valero Refining, Port Arthur Refinery 250 000
Calcasieu Refining Co, Lake Charles Refinery 30 000
Premcor Refining Inc, Port Arthur Refinery 255 000
Citgo Petro, Lake Charles Refinery 324 300
Valero Refining Co, Krptz Spring Refinery 80 000
Placid Refining Co, Port Allen Refinery 48 500
ExxonMobil, Baton Rouge Refinery 493 500
Motiva Enterprises LLC, Convent Refinery 235 000
Marathon Ashland Petroleum LLC, Garyville Refinery 245 000
Valero, Saint Charles Refinery 185 000
Shell Chem LP, Saint Rose Refinery 55 000
ConcoPhilips, Belle Chasse Refinery 247 000
Chevron, Pascagoula Refinery 325 000
Trigeant EP LTD, Mobile Refinery 16 700

Saudi Arabia 1 467 000   Iraq 410 000
Mexico 1 022 000   Kuwait 319 000
Venezuela 901 000   Brazil 283 000
Russia 468   Angola 229 000
Colombia 459   United Kingdom 156 000

58

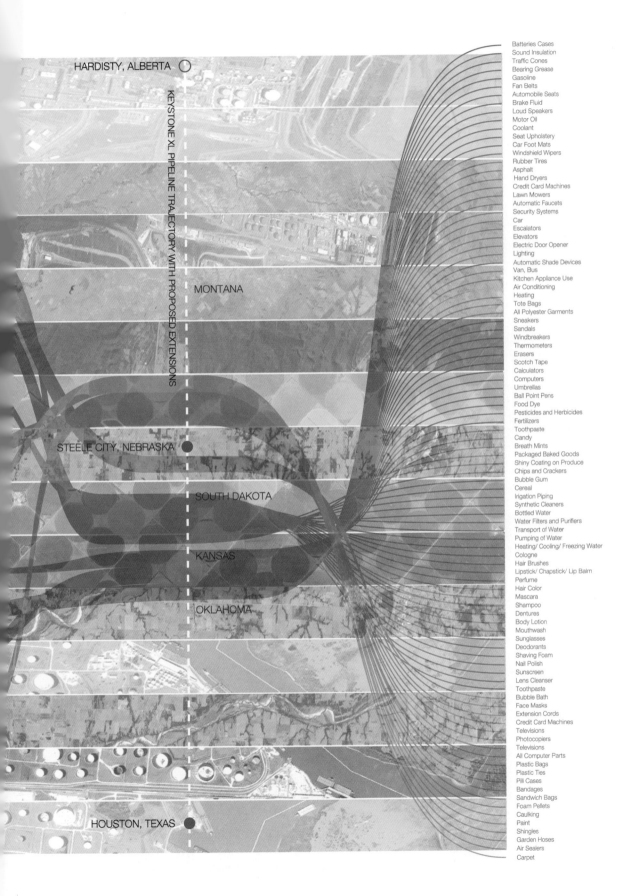

HARDISTY, ALBERTA

KEYSTONE XL PIPELINE TRAJECTORY WITH PROPOSED EXTENSIONS

MONTANA

STEELE CITY, NEBRASKA

SOUTH DAKOTA

KANSAS

OKLAHOMA

HOUSTON, TEXAS

Batteries Cases
Sound Insulation
Traffic Cones
Bearing Grease
Gasoline
Fan Belts
Automobile Seats
Brake Fluid
Loud Speakers
Motor Oil
Coolant
Seat Upholstery
Car Foot Mats
Windshield Wipers
Rubber Tires
Asphalt
Hand Dryers
Credit Card Machines
Lawn Mowers
Automatic Faucets
Security Systems
Car
Escalators
Elevators
Electric Door Opener
Lighting
Automatic Shade Devices
Van, Bus
Kitchen Appliance Use
Air Conditioning
Heating
Tote Bags
All Polyester Garments
Sneakers
Sandals
Windbreakers
Thermometers
Erasers
Scotch Tape
Calculators
Computers
Umbrellas
Ball Point Pens
Food Dye
Pesticides and Herbicides
Fertilizers
Toothpaste
Candy
Breath Mints
Packaged Baked Goods
Shiny Coating on Produce
Chips and Crackers
Bubble Gum
Cereal
Irrigation Piping
Synthetic Cleaners
Bottled Water
Water Filters and Purifiers
Transport of Water
Pumping of Water
Heating/ Cooling/ Freezing Water
Cologne
Hair Brushes
Lipstick/ Chapstick/ Lip Balm
Perfume
Hair Color
Mascara
Shampoo
Dentures
Body Lotion
Mouthwash
Sunglasses
Deodorants
Shaving Foam
Nail Polish
Sunscreen
Lens Cleanser
Toothpaste
Bubble Bath
Face Masks
Extension Cords
Credit Card Machines
Televisions
Photocopiers
Televisions
All Computer Parts
Plastic Bags
Plastic Ties
Pill Cases
Bandages
Sandwich Bags
Foam Pellets
Caulking
Paint
Shingles
Garden Hoses
Air Sealers
Carpet

sources of water. But landscape architects needn't confined to only designing and building landscape When it comes to the invisibilities of the pipeline could, for example, design and visualize a source-tracking system that could disclose exactly how much energy was required to grow the juicy, red apple you're eating from which company the energy was produced, and exactly how it was created. This system could be applied to produce, seafood, poultry, items of clothing, building materials, and plants. This would empower the consumer to make an educated choice about their consumption patterns and enable them to understand how even the most seemingly inconsequential choice ripples outward with social, ecological and spatial consequences around the world. Twenty-first century landscape architecture in the context of contemporary, environmental, political economic, and social issues will need to be regarded as an agent beyond cleaning, dusting and decorating the path of industry to becoming the interface through which people are connected to aspects of the infrastructural landscape upon which they directly rely.

The immense complexity and sheer scale of energy production and resource consumption would appear, on the surface, to be an issue that lies outside the realm of expertise of landscape architecture. But expanding interests and ambitions within the field have shifted the scope of the discipline to engage with the matter of resources and energy consumption on varying levels. However, beyond interest and ambition, I believe that a sense of responsibility and duty lie at the foundation and that the discipline should be fully invested in engaging with issues and opportunities that revolve around energy resources and pipelines on physical, socio-cultural and communicative levels. As infrastructural systems multiply and spread out over the landscape bifurcating towns, cities, and mega-regions, landscape architecture will need to act as the interface through which resources of energy meets the human sphere of physicality and in so doing, substantially alter our understanding of the infrastructural environment upon which we depend.

Reference

Government of Alberta, "Alberta's Oil Sands. Opportunity. Balance." ast modified 03 01, 2008. Accessed November 23, 2013. http://www. nvironment.alberta.ca/documents/Oil_Sands_Opportunity_Balance. df.

"Tar Sands and the Carbon Numbers." The New York Times, The)pinion Pages edition, sec. Editorials, August 29, 2011. http://www. ytimes.com/2011/08/22/opinion/tar-sands-and-the-carbon-numbers. tml?_r=0 (accessed September 14, 2013).

, The TransCanada Corporation, "Route Map." Last modified July 21, .013. Accessed September 14, 2013. http://www.transcanada.com/ ndex.html

4 US Geological Survey, "High Plains Regional Groundwater Study – High Plains aquifer system." Last modified April 29, 2013. Accessed September 14, 2013. http://co.water.usgs.gov/nawqa/hpgw/HPGW_ 1ome.html.

5 Carwardine Peter, (VP Land & Corporate Development at OMERS Energy Inc. President at Baycrest Energy Ltd.), interview by Shafir, Michael Ockrant , "Landscape Architects and Pipelines," October 2013.

6 Chevron Corporation, "Chevron in Canada- How Does an Oil Refin-ery Work?." Accessed September 14, 2013. http://www.chevron.ca/ operations/refining/refineryworks.asp.

7 Udo Weilacher, Syntax of Landscape, The Landscape Architecture of Peter Latz and Partners, (Berlin: Birkhäuser, 2008).

8 Carwardine, Peter, (VP Land & Corporate Development at OMERS Energy Inc. President at Baycrest Energy Ltd.), interview by Shafir, Michael Ockrant, 18 September 2013.
8 The Oxford Dictionary, "Definition and Etymology of Resource." Accessed August 29, 2013. http://oxforddictionaries.com/us/defini-tion/american_english/resource?q=resource.

8 Lewis Mumford, The Brown Decades: A Study of the Arts in Ameri-ca, 1865-1895, (New York: Dover Publications, 1931).

10 Karl Marx, "Capital. A Critique of Political Economy," The Process of Production of Capital, Vol. Book 1, ed. Frederick Engels (Moscow: Progress Publishers, 1887)http://www.marxists.org/archive/marx/ works/download/pdf/Capital-Volume-I.pdf (accessed November 23, 2013).

11 Kate Orff, and Richard Misrach, Petrochemical America, (New York: Aperture, 2012).

Joanna Karaman describes a spatial sequence of the Dutch sea infrastructure by questioning the role of the user. A place designed for populations but not for 'people'.

[rise]

An Outing to the Dutch Seafront

Joanna Karaman

> "When you want to be alone, you can sneak away along the bottom. And when you feel good and strong, you saunter proudly along the crest, and then the boys whistle at you. I still think of that dike as an old friend."
>
> – Marije Tilstra; Royal Haskoning DHV, Landscape architect[1]

Questions such as where a structure sits and how it relates to the collective memory of the people whose lives it affects is a train of thought that personifies infrastructure. The Dutch coastline not only unveils a wide range of defenses, but also the nuances of the places they create. In the Netherlands, these coastal defenses are an integral part of the country's historic landscape. However, the newer generation takes the protection for granted, often forgetting previous floods and vulnerabilities. Thus the matter gets pushed to the periphery of the country's culture. Dikes and polders that once were central gathering points of Dutch villages today lie buried beneath highways and outside the memories of many of the nearby residents. Flood protection has been quantified to the extent that its construction practically precludes or marginalizes the feeling of community and the human scale. "Safety has become something for the engineers, we increasingly rely on them...but we don't get a sense of what it's about."[2]

Therefore, I ventured to the Dutch coast, to these structures, to see for myself. What follows is an account of what I encountered, what I saw.

Arms, weighing 680 tons, rotate around a ball and socket joint embedded in a colossal foundation block of 52,000 tons. The appendages, each as long as the Eifel Tower, swing around a fixed axis.[3] From the nearby ground, none of this appears evident. This is primarily because the choreography is only enacted as needed, triggered to close when a storm surge greater than three meters is anticipated.

This is the Maeslantkering storm surge barrier. For one of the largest moving structures on earth, the stakes are quite high – it stands in the middle of a major shipping route and protects one of the busiest ports in Europe, Rotterdam.[4] The Maeslantkering opened in 1997 after six years of construction, costing 660 million Euros ($902 million USD).[5] The gates were not activated until November 2007, and they continue to stand at the ready, awaiting the worst.

From the coast, visitors peer across the metal grates to a single billboard that describes the mechanics of the structure. A wire fence limits access and proximity. All the while, the gates lie flat and low, with a sublime discreetness that fools no one but the engineers.

On the road preceding the Maeslantkering, a colonnade of wind turbines beckons the potential avid recreationalist. Signs advertise a new park for skateboarding, rambling, ship watching, and even children's birthday parties. Yet for now, even on a sunny summer day, the barrier and its adjacent peninsula park remains primarily vacant.

The Maeslantkering is the youngest of the 13 barriers collectively called the Delta Works. They stand as the Dutch response to the catastrophic North Sea Flood of 1953, a reaction that required 30 years to finally see to fruition.[6] Moving south into the province of Zeeland, lies the largest of these barriers, the Oosterscheldekring. The 9km wall is set on concrete pillars weighing 18,000 tons each, along with approximately sixty 40m wide steel doors. Due to its staggering scale, the American Society of Civil Engineers has identified this structure as one of the seven wonders of the modern world.[7] The structure, however, has had mixed public support. Halfway through its construction, conservationists called for the opening up of the gates to preserve the saline environment. The compromise was that the Oosterscheldekring would remain open most of the time, but would close when there was a risk of a water invasion.[8]

Despite these environmental and water quality considerations, the area around the barrier is primarily hardscape – vast and barren. In lieu of trees, giant wind turbines mark the territory. Walking through this landscape on a clear sunny day, I can't help but think of how different the area would look mid-storm. Could a single structure, as stout as it may seem, really keep out the power of the ocean, the storm surge?

In the face of the imposing immensity of this engineered landscape, the area still seems active in the good weather. There is a sprinkling of cyclists, campers, and even a water park and education center nearby. The Dutch public uses the space in spite of its lack of invitation.

I continued my trek at the northern tip of the Netherlands through Texel, the barrier island that stands in the front line to the North Sea. The island itself has historically stood as a gateway to the country. During the Golden Age of the early 17th century, over 3000 ships from the Dutch East India company would journey through the passage between the mainland and the island.[9]

Today, Wadenzee that stands behind the island harbors mudflats and bird nesting grounds. Tides get so low here that the shallow waters have cultivated a culture of beachcombing, attracting wanderers and treasure hunters from near and far. The island was once comprised of two separate land bodies that were poldered together in the 17th century. When the polders were breached one hundred years later, the defense was never reinstated, and the small island coast was left to the whims of the North Sea.[10]

And so the island's failure became its new defense, removing most waterfront human inhabitation. The tenuous rift of the breach greets meanderers with the pungent scent of salt water and muck along the path to the waterfront. Small villages lay nested inland within the dune buffer, but citizens are isolated. Accessible only by the occasional ferry, migrating birds come and go with greater ease.

This coast was documented in 1971 by the Dutch cultural figures Godfriend Bomans and Jan Wolkers, who created a radio show about their week walking on the island. At the end of their show, one moved to the island, while the other fell into depression.[11]

The monotony of the place is relentless.

Here, the sea comes and goes as it pleases – it has an empty canvas stretching over a mile long. Wide expanses of grasses and pickerelweed proliferate along the vast beach. The island's sprawling dunescape, the remnants of past fortifications, envelop me as I move through rolling hills of sand and shrub towards the sea. Staring out towards the flatness of the sea, the traces of dunes are at my back. I am alone in this unfamiliar terrain, my feet sunk into at least a foot of mud. I have never felt so small. With each step I hardly gain any ground. But I'm not here to cover distance, I'm here to move through time. I'm here to grasp a glimpse of the future, to understand the scale of the sea.

As much as dikes and polders can speak of the Dutch identity, they themselves may be a flood protection measure of the past. No new dikes or polders have been built in the Netherlands since the end of World War II. In fact, beginning in the 1990s many of the polders have been opened and allowed to flood, blurring the sharp lines originally made by the construction of the structures.[12] In the case of the Delta Works Projects, the colossal sea walls are impossible to camouflage, except perhaps in the cultural consciousness of the Dutch. Today, few Dutch citizens get close to the barriers. The drama of their construction seems to have faded since the project's completion in the late 1990s. For most, the rigid geometries and imposing sense of resistance are out of sight, out of mind.

In addition to the impending danger of floods, another more immediate consequence of living beneath sea level is that salt water relentlessly seeps in, under and around the engineered solutions. In fact, the Dutch use the majority of their freshwater reserves to rinse the encroaching salt away. In the Rijnland region alone (the area of the Netherlands that constitutes the bulk of its GDP) at least 9 billion liters are used for this flushing each year.[13] In reaction to this uneconomical practice, a movement is emerging for a calculated re-integration with the saline environment. If further engineering is required to ameliorate and protect an already thoroughly engineered system, was the rigor of its construction necessary? Or does the integrated approach truly need a rigid backbone from which to grow?

To these rhetorical questions, I merely add my own observations.

References

1 Tracy Metz, and Maartje van den Heuvel, Sweet & Salt: Water and the Dutch, (Rotterdam: NAi Publishers, 2012), 79.

2 Ibid.

3 The Delta Project: Preserving the environment and securing Zeeland against flooding, (Burgh-Haamstede, Zeeland: Deltapark Neeltje Jans and Florad Marketing Group, 2012), 32.

4 Stijn Reinhard, and Henk Folmer, Water policy in the Netherlands integrated management in a densely populated delta, (Washington DC: Resources for the Future, 2009), 23-43.

5 The Delta Project: Preserving the environment and securing Zeeland against flooding, (Burgh-Haamstede, Zeeland: Deltapark Neeltje Jans and Florad Marketing Group, 2012), 6-9.

6 Ibid, 16-22.

7 ASCE: American Society of Civil Engineers, "The Seven Wonders of the Modern World." Last modified 2013. Accessed Setember 28, 2013. http://www.asce.org.

8 H.L.F. Saeijs, and Paul Karis, Turning the Tide: Essays on Dutch Ways with Water, (Delft: VSSD, 2008), 57-62.

9 Tracy Metz, and Maartje van den Heuvel, Sweet & Salt: Water and the Dutch, (Rotterdam: NAi Publishers, 2012), 150.

10 Stijn Reinhard, and Henk Folmer, Water policy in the Netherlands integrated management in a densely populated delta, (Washington DC: Resources for the Future, 2009), 57-61.

11 Tracy Metz, and Maartje van den Heuvel, Sweet & Salt: Water and the Dutch, (Rotterdam: NAi Publishers, 2012), 223.

12 H.L.F. Saeijs, and Paul Karis, Turning the Tide: Essays on Dutch Ways with Water, (Delft: VSSD, 2008), 28-48.

13 Tracy Metz, and Maartje van den Heuvel, Sweet & Salt: Water and the Dutch, (Rotterdam: NAi Publishers, 2012), 77.

What is the role of landscape architecture in the extraction of natural gas? Anneliza Carmalt Kaufer begins this investigation by understanding what role, if any, can be had through the process of fracking.

[extract]

What the Frack?
Anneliza Carmalt Kaufer

The United States of America possesses the largest proven recoverable unconventional gas[1] reserve in the world[2]. These resources are expected to meet 30% of the total national electricity demand by 2035[3] and have the capacity to supply the country with cheap energy for at least 100 years.[4] The Marcellus shale formation lying beneath Ohio, Pennsylvania and New York is the largest of these basins and is the focus of current fracking activity within the United States.

I grew up in the rural northeastern portion of Pennsylvania where the low, eroded Appalachians and bucolic landscape, dotted with dairy farms, comprise a region known as the Endless Mountains. Recently, it has been the setting for a documentary film called Gasland and memoirs such as Seamus McGraw's *End of Country,* so maybe it's doomed to be called something else by now. In the past, trying to describe where I'm from to people unfamiliar with the area often resulted in an offhand, "You wouldn't know it. It's in the middle of nowhere." Today, it is most definitely on the map, as the epicenter of one of the world's richest shale gas formations[5] and the infamous means of its extraction: fracking.[6]

Bradford County and Susquehanna County are situated in the northeast corner of Pennsylvania in the Susquehanna River watershed, which drains south to the Chesapeake Bay. Both counties are designated as "rural" by the Center for Rural Pennsylvania, with respective population densities of 55 and 53 persons per square mile.[7] They are also ranked first and second in the state for the number of oil and gas wells permitted and drilled (through the process of fracking), with 2,646 permitted wells (1,124 drilled) on 663 sites in Bradford County and 1,486 permitted wells (835 drilled) on 415 sites in Susquehanna County.[8] The sheer number alone is astounding, but when chronologically paired[9] with the onset of America's Great Recession, the presence of the natural gas industry in this region was ubiquitous.

County residents experience these impacts and their magnitude differently, but you are hard-pressed to find someone with no story to tell, from the drive home on a now traffic-jammed dirt road[10] to the neighbor's well-water that can be lit on fire straight from the spigot.[11] And while I can think of the same in my own experience, I want to focus on two stories that helped impel my investigation on fracking: the first is the story of the Lottery Winner and the second, the Contentious Objector.

My extended families collectively own two properties in Susquehanna County. The first is a 125-acre property that my in-laws previously farmed. Now, agricultural production is limited to supplying neighboring dairy farmers with hay. The oil and gas lease was signed in 2008 for $2,000 per acre with 15% royalties. This was before the crisis at Dimock,[12] a town four miles up the road, reached mainstream media and alerted the country to the potential negative consequences of fracking. The gas company and their engineers compiled a development plan that shows two future pads, one 3.5 acres and the other 2 acres, both graded into the hillside above the house and accessed by two new roads that connect to the existing dirt road at the base of the hill. A pipeline easement for the Williams Voyager Pipeline bisects the property with a 50-foot swath and connects to the interstate Tennessee Pipeline along the northern edge of Springville Township.

The second property consists of 700 acres of primarily second-growth forest. A 40-acre lake lies in the center, surrounded by approximately 300 acres of its undeveloped catchment. When energy companies approached my family in 2009, they offered $5,500 per acre with 20% royalties. Cautious of detriment to the property's most valuable asset (the lake) my family proceeded to research the process of fracking in an effort to learn about and avoid what we feared could be disaster. As a family of foresters, planners, engineers, lawyers, and concerned landowners, we compiled a lease that was designed to protect the land and reduce potential disturbance while still attempting to manage the practicalities of the established fracking process. In the end, the energy companies decided the property was not feasible for natural gas extraction and discontinued negotiations.

This retraction could have resulted from a host of reasons including global supply and demand trends for natural gas, unfavorable seismic results testing natural gas potential, or because our demands would complicate their standard procedures and reduce their profit margins. Whatever the reason, the comparison of these experiences prompted me to question the adaptability of the extraction process to unique site characteristics and individual landowners. Landscape architecture prides itself on sensitivity to site specificity, which, in turn, led me to question the possibilities of landscape architecture's role in the fracking industry. What is the potential for our profession, as supposed stewards of the environment, regarding this economically rational and rapacious enterprise?

An Exploration in Unfamiliar Extraction

The fracking process begins when the landowner signs a lease with the energy company that gives rights to extract oil, gas and/or minerals from the property. Initially, seismic testing shows the potential for gas extraction and the specific well alignment needed to optimize gas return.[13] At this time, the landowner should also contract an independent company to perform baseline water testing for drinking water and any surface water that may exist on the property.

The energy company then constructs a well pad, which is approximately five acres of cleared, flat ground.[14] A pad of this size has the ultimate capacity for six wells, reaching a drainage footprint of one square mile. Sometimes only two wells are drilled and fracked at once, potentially extending the timeline of pad occupation to decades. Interim reclamation is required by the Pennsylvania Department of Environmental Protection (PA DEP) if this practice occurs.[15] Drilling begins with a rotary rig boring a hole 3,000 to 8,000 feet deep before extending up to 5,000 feet horizontally underground. A series of cement and steel casings are used to line the drill hole and protect the surrounding aquifer from contamination. After drilling, the well is fracked. In order to release the natural gas that is trapped in the Marcellus shale, dynamite is dropped into the drill hole and detonated in stages along the length of the well.[16] Following the explosions, three to five million gallons of water,[17] mixed with sand and 596 chemicals[18] is pumped at extremely high pressures to open the fissures and allow the gas to flow to the surface. This mixture includes anti-corrosive chemicals to protect the drill bit and well casing, viscosity-adjusting chemicals that lubricate and promote gas flow, and antibacterial chemicals to reduce growth of naturally occurring bacteria that can clog the fissures in the shale. The sand acts to prop open these fissures and allows for a more continuous flow.

After fracking, the internal geologic pressure pushes the fluid out of the well where separators siphon gas into gathering pipelines for distribution and water into collection and storage areas.

Along with the original chemicals that were pumped into the well, the flowback water contains high salt content from the shale formation as well as normally occurring radioactive material, such as barium and strontium.[19] Various methods exist for treatment and disposal of this fluid, also called "produced water."

In an 'open system', flowback is stored in open impoundments on site. The size of these ponds can vary, but the associated disturbance averages about 10 acres.[20] Produced water is stored in these open ponds, exposed to unknowing wildlife and unpredictable precipitation[21], until it evaporates or is transported to a designated waste facility. In the more common 'closed system', flowback is stored in closed tanks on-site before being transported and recycled in the fracking of other wells, or to designated wastewater treatment facilities or deep injection wells.[22] In some cases, a closed system permits open container storage, but restricts fluid levels to only half-full.[23] Water flows to the surface for duration of the well's lifespan, but ultimately only 10% to 30% is recovered.[24] Each well can be fracked up to 18 times[25] in an effort to sustain the flow and pressure of natural gas. This frequency compounds the need for massive amounts of water. Gas flows from the well through gathering pipelines, to compressor stations, where an energy intensive and loud process increases the pressure in order to flow into larger distribution lines, such as the Tennessee Pipeline. This network of pipelines is delineated by a 50-foot cleared swath, replanted with meadow grass for what is, essentially, perpetuity.[26]

After a well pad is completed (i.e., all six wells are fracked and in production), the PA DEP requires a final remediation effort. The well head, separator, and water tanks remain within a one to two acre cleared lawn area that continues to be accessed for maintenance and water collection via the original access road. The remainder of the pad is restored to the original land use, whether field or forest. More permanent best management practices are implemented to deal with changed runoff conditions and water quality. A typical gas well remains in production for 15 to 20 years. At this time, the well is plugged and abandoned and the lease is terminated, returning the land to the property owner.[27]

Opportunity Calls

The American Society of Landscape Architects has yet to release an official national policy regarding the role of landscape architecture in relation to fracking.[28] This is problematic because fracking radically impacts both the cultural and ecological landscape. On the one hand, fracking offers the United States a greater degree of global energy independence and creates wealth for individual landowners. On the other, it brings a boom and bust cycle to otherwise stable rural economies and re-engineers the landscape at both local and regional scales. Fracking may prove to be toxic or it may not. As it has in other industrial processes, will landscape architecture again play the role of post-extraction cleaner, or can we engage with the process as it happens?

My research indicates that landscape architects currently have little involvement with fracking; working neither with nor against the industry. This lack of action may be due to the infancy of the industry and the focus on well pad negotiations, permitting and development.[29] It can be assumed that our role could adapt to suit the shifting demands of the industry, yet this still places landscape architects in the reactive position. Some landscape architects do find the capacity for involvement, though their role is typically limited to small-scale, topical interventions such as erosion and sediment control plans or retroactive cleanup activity such as interim pad restoration.[30] Research occurring through the design programs at Pennsylvania State University[31] and Cornell University that attempts spatial and infrastructural planning, as well as innovative ways to deal with habitat fragmentation, should not be discounted. Operating along pipeline infrastructure is one subject of such research, both in terms of configuration strategies based on various priority scenarios,[32] and buffering and habitat connections. In contrast, engineers and planners have established themselves as critical actors with a significant presence in industry.[33] The influence of these professions is seen from the design of the pervasive infrastructural networks laid by the industry to planning and policy impacting rural communities with expanding economies.

If we accept fracking and its concomitant infrastructure as a given (and it would appear that to do otherwise is futile), how can we critically respond to the current modus operandi of the industry and expand our role and methods of operation? This is not a problem of competition between landscape architects and other consultants, but a question of disciplinary scope and relevance.

Can Landscape Infrastructure serve as a relevant theory in this capacity, or is our profession merely perpetuating a fetish for power and system organization that leads to more discourse and inaction? Claimed as the true alliance between civil engineering and landscape architecture,[34] Landscape Infrastructure could warrant the disciplinary scope and relevance for which we are searching. Pierre Bélanger suggests simplifying our approach to infrastructure as the basic system of essential services that can structure a city, nation or region and shape future growth. It is essential, in this case, to broaden our definition of landscape beyond the conventional "biotic" or "green" to include within our purview entire socio-economic processes impacting upon regional landscapes. This, along with much of the bravado of landscape urbanism in recent years, suggests that landscape architects should at least attempt to anticipate the design of industrial infrastructures to ensure that the deleterious consequence of their implementation is minimized. This is easier said than done, but if we are not involved, then nothing can be either said or done.

Furthermore, if we look to Lateral Office's pamphlet architecture, Coupling, the idea of using latent yet pervasive infrastructural systems as a framework or "site" for new services or distribution is a helpful way to imagine a future for this region after fracking is obsolete and the inevitable bust has occurred.[35] Can the disturbance associated with the development and continued use of this infrastructure actually be reinterpreted as an asset? Can we pre-emptively temper this bust by rethinking this existing infrastructure now as a way to frame an alternative economy, or at least a more diverse one, in the future? Natural gas is often lauded for being the transitional fuel for our country's foray into renewable energy production.[36] Can this alternative economy mentioned above be based on the development and distribution of such an alternative and renewable energy system? Or are there other systems or services more suited to couple with

this energy infrastructure? Can this method provide an appropriate way to structure phases of new growth as we begin to think more into the future than the terms of the current industry? To operate systemically, this idea is not complete with only a regional framework plan and must be balanced by site-specific design strategies, as explored by Alan Berger in *Systemic Design Can Change the World.* [37]

Additionally, landscape architects can play an educative role. In *Petrochemical America,* Kate Orff explores the "eco-portrait"[38] as an innovative representational technique to explore the territory of Louisiana's Cancer Alley and the spatial and non-spatial interdependencies therein. By synthesizing mapping and analysis, Orff specifically targets and provokes design professionals to imagine new potentials for design within territories of extraction. Similarly, Rania Ghosn frames energy and systems in *Common Interests* by conflating the landscape of production with the landscape of consumption to expose contradictions or weakness in a clearer way for the general public. It is an attempt to suggest interventions that may avert disasters without allowing process flow diagrams to disconnect these two environments. [39]

While the validity of these representational methods is not in question, such a level of engagement remains largely aesthetic. Several gaps in the field present straightforward paths of action for our discipline. Dr. David Velinsky, the vice president for environmental research at the Patrick Center for Environmental Research of the University of Pennsylvania, calls for a cumulative impact study in *The Marcellus Shale Play* rather than the piecemeal research performed to date.[40] As a discipline of generalists, landscape architects could undertake holistic research into the fracking phenomenon. A scenario-based design study, particularly one embedded in a local community's values, could investigate the pros and cons of different degrees of design intervention at various stages and various scales of the fracking process.

Whatever the mode of operation, the time for involvement is now. The extraction of natural gas from Marcellus shale is an industry that is growing and evolving. It will do so without us if we wait for an invitation to the table.

References

1 Unconventional gas is gas that is embedded in the source material (in this case shale), as opposed to conventional gas, which exists as a reservoir and is independent from the material around it. "Unconventional Natural Gas Resources," NaturalGas.Org, accessed on Nov 12, 2013, http://www.naturalgas.org/overview/unconvent_ng_resource.asp.

2 "Fracking: Frequently Asked Questions," Intellectual Takeout: Feed Your Mind, accessed on Nov 22, 2013, http://www.intellectualtakeout.org/faqs/fracking-frequently-asked-questions-faq.

3 US Energy Information Administration, Annual Energy Outlook 2013: with projections to 2040 (Washington DC: Office of Integrated and International Energy Analysis, 2013), 4.

4 "Why Natural Gas: Abundant," UGI: Energy to do More, accessed on November 4, 2013, http://www.ugi.com/portal/page/portal/UGI/Residential_Gas/Why_Abundant.

5 Identified by geologist, Terry Engelder of Pennsylvania State University in 2007: Brian Orland, et al., "Effects of Marcellus Shale Gas Development on Environment and Health," Lecture, Association of Collegiate Schools of Planning, Salt Lake City, Oct 13, 2011.

6 'Fracking' refers to the High Volume Horizontal Hydraulic Fracturing drilling method.

7 The 2010 US Census found the average population density for Pennsylvania as 284 persons/mi2. Anything below this classifies as rural. Bradford and Susquehanna Counties are among the 25% most rural counties in Pennsylvania. "Rural/Urban PA," The Center for Rural Pennsylvania, accessed on October 10, 2013, http://www.rural.palegislature.us/rural_urban.html#maps.

8 "County Map & Permit Tables," MarcellusGas.Org, accessed Nov 19, 2013, http://www.marcellusgas.org.

9 The first unconventional gas well in Pennsylvania was drilled in 2005. Brian Orland, "Effects of Marcellus Shale Gas Development on Environment and Health."

10 It is estimated that each well requires approximately 1,000 individual truck trips for materials, water and waste disposal. "Our Look at Gas Drilling Truck Traffic," Marcellus-Shale.us, accessed on November 22, 2013, http://www.marcellus-shale.us/truck-traffic.htm.

11 Josh Fox, "Gasland," Documentary, Directed by Josh Fox, HBO, 2010, DVD.

12 In reference to Norma Fiorentino's back yard water well that exploded on January 1, 2009 after drilling occurred a few hundred yards away. "Dimock, PA: Ground Zero in the Fight over Fracking" NPR: State Impact, accessed November 20, 2013, http://stateimpact.npr.org/pennsylvania/tag/dimock/.

13 Typically this is a northeast-southwest orientation in this region. Brian Orland, "Effects of Marcellus Shale Gas Development on Environment and Health."

14 Ibid.

15 Talisman Energy Inc. via Joseph Katruska and Laura Frano, telephone interview with author, November 21, 2013.

16 David Velinsky, "The Marcellus Shale Play: Environmental Impact of Drilling for Natural Gas in the Marcellus Shale" Lecture, Perelman School of Medicine/CEET, University of Pennsylvania, Philadelphia, September 15, 2011.

17 "Explore Shale," Public Media for Public Understanding, accessed November 22, 2013, http://exploreshale.org/.

18 The exact chemical makeup is unknown because gas companies are exempt from all or parts of the following federal regulations: Clean Water Act, Clean Air Act, Resource Conservation and Recovery Act, Comprehensive Environmental Response, Compensation and Liability Act and the Safe Drinking Water Act and all or parts of the following state regulations: Scenic Rivers Act, Safe Drinking Water Act, Air Pollution Control Act, Floodplain Management Act and Oil and Gas Act 13 (exempts them from some zoning requirements). Brian Orland and Timothy Murtha, "Marcellus Matters: How communities and landscapes are shaped," Pennsylvania State University, accessed Oct 10, 2013, http://marcellusbydesign.psu.edu/.

19 "Our Look at Gas Drilling Wastewater," Marcellus-Shale.us, accessed on November 22, 2013, http://www.marcellus-shale.us/truck-traffic.htm.

20 Brian Orland, "Effects of Marcellus Shale Gas Development on Environment and Health."

21 Well pads were flooded throughout Bradford County during Tropical Storm Lee in 2011.

22 Initially, produced water was taken to standard wastewater treatment plants that did not have the capacity to treat for chemicals and radioactive waste present in this fluid. Antiquated regulations did not limit concentrations of these contaminants at wastewater discharge points. "Our Look at Gas Drilling Wastewater." Deep injection wells in Youngstown, OH have been linked to increased seismic activity in the region. Choi, Charles Q., "Fracking Practices to Blame for Ohio Earthquakes," LiveScience, accessed on October 15, 2013, http://www.livescience.com/39406-fracking-wasterwater-injection-caused-ohio-earthquakes.html.

23 Chesapeake Energy Corporation, Interview by Carmalt family, Chesapeake satellite office, Towanda, Pennsylvania, April 23, 2010.

24 Because the majority of fracking fluid remains underground, the fracking process requires continuous freshwater input. "Environmental Impacts Associated with Hydraulic Fracturing," The Network for Public Health Law, accessed on November 23, 2013, https://www.networkforphl.org/_asset/w74j2w/.

25 Fox, Josh, "Gasland," Documentary, Directed by Josh Fox, HBO, 2010, DVD.

26 Interview with Joseph Katruska and Laura Frano.

27 Ibid.

28 ASLA plans to provide a public statement and policy on natural gas extraction and fracking in 2014. McKee, Bradford, email message to the author via ASLA Government Affairs, October 16, 2013.

29 Interview with Joseph Katruska and Laura Frano.

30 Landscape architects are licensed to create erosion and sediment control plans through the PA DEP. Gilliland, Donald, "Landscape Architects Find New Business in Marcellus Shale," PennLive, accessed on October 23, 2013, http://www.pennlive.com/midstate/index.ssf/2011/04/landscape_architects_find_new.html. and Kim Sorvig, "Welcome to Frackville," Landscape Architecture Magazine, Vol 103 No 6 (2013): 87. and Interview with Joseph Katruska and Laura Frano.

31 "Marcellus By Design," Pennsylvania State University, accessed Oct 10, 2013, http://marcellusbydesign.psu.edu/.

32 Priority scenarios: shortest distance, market-driven, conservation. Brian Orland and Timothy Murtha, "Marcellus Matters: Informing and engaging citizens in community planning," accessed Oct 10, 2013, http://marcellusbydesign.psu.edu/.

33 Elaine Jardin, County Planning Director with Tioga Investigates Natural Gas, Telephone interview, October 16, 2013.

34 Pierre Bélanger, "Landscape Infrastructure: Urbanism beyond Engineering" (PhD. diss., Wageningen University, 2013).

35 Susan Christopherson, "The Economic Consequences of Marcellus Shale Gas Extraction: Key Issues," CaRDI Reports 14 (2011): 4.

36 Katia Balassiano, "Tackling 'Wicked Problems' in Planning Studio Courses," Journal of Planning Education and Research 31(4) (2011): 454.

37 Alan Berger, Systemic Design Can Change the World, (Amsterdam: SUN Publishers, 2009) 36.

38 Orff defines eco-portrait as "synthetic moments where a series of data points and observations converge into an overall ecology or process view, joining seemingly isolated phenomena into a perceptible whole" when defining maps (orientation), data narratives (analysis), and eco-portrait. Richard Misrach and Kate Orff, Petrochemical America (New York: Aperture, 2012), 117.

39 Rania Ghosn, "Where are the Missing Spaces? The Geography of some Uncommon Interests," Perspecta 45: Agency (2012) 109–116.

40 David Velinsky, "The Marcellus Shale Play: Environmental Impact of Drilling for Natural Gas in the Marcellus Shale." Lecture, 2011.

Anooshey Rahim investigates areas of neglect in urban areas as consequences of debilitating landscapes.

[empower]

The Spatial Dimension of Inequality

Anooshey Rahim

In highly urbanized contexts, certain populations are pushed to areas of spatial neglect such as near landfills, in flood plains, and downstream of effluent-producing factories. Areas of disinvestment in cities around the world are inevitably juxtaposed with areas of steady investment, where access to design and new technologies is the status quo. This inequity manifests in many ways: high versus low, wet versus dry, hard versus soft, close versus far, safe versus dangerous, and facilitating versus debilitating.

Large areas of underutilized space, too little green space, vacancy, physical barriers, and brownfields are examples of socially debilitating landscape features. The presence and interaction of these features devitalizes the socio-economic health of neighborhoods.

In *Place Matters: Metropolitics for the 21st Century,* Peter Dreir points out that while city officials and researchers actively debate the reasons for the growing social disparities in the United States, they have paid little attention to the spatial or physical dimensions of inequality. Dreir's argument is that place matters because it exerts a strong influence on our choices and on our quality of life; affecting access to jobs, public services, shopping, culture and personal security.[1] Randolph T. Hester, landscape architect and commentator on community development and participatory planning, calls this 'ecological democracy'. He explains that "[f]orm matters to ecological democracy. City form influences our daily lives. City form concretizes our values and reflects them back to us."[2]

According to Hester "fairness" in city design can be measured by studying the degrees of accessibility, inclusion and equity in any given area.[3] These three registers of fairness are reflected in both the physical and nonphysical landscape of the city. The presence of reasonable accessibility, inclusivity and equity creates a facilitating landscape with opportunity, security and a working economy. The absence of any of these conditions creates a debilitating landscape: a place with barriers, little investment, and manifesting in a demoralized community.

In order to approach the issue of urban spatial inequality it is important to recognize three factors: the existence of a spatial dimension that correlates to non-physical social inequality; the differing design parameters of a facilitating landscape in contrast to those of a debilitating landscape; and the need to reevaluate the role of the designer and the way design services are applied. Because of a common lack of resources, design in debilitating landscapes requires an approach that is different to the orthodox design and delivery of landscape architectural services. By virtue of its sensitivity to context, landscape architecture is well suited to working closely with marginalized communities. Landscape architecture has the capacity to catalyze change towards a more equitable future.

If spatial inequality engenders social disparity, then design and community galvanization can create opportunity and empowerment. A trans-disciplinary design method can enable communities to create, operate and maintain their local infrastructures, address debilitating features and claim ownership of new initiatives. A push for local infrastructures provides an opportunity for community engagement at a scale where issues are likely to engage more residents, unlike city-wide projects which often require relatively anonymous, large scale, top-down measures.[4]

Landscape architects are important agents of "connectedness" because of their ability to foster and facilitate relationships between community members, designers, local institutions, city officials and developers, while designing with an imagination that links the ecological environment of a place with community values. In the debilitating landscape the landscape architect must inspire and collaborate with community groups and act as a political and entrepreneurial catalyst. As such the very notion of design moves from the production of aesthetics to active design agency in complex networks of socio-economic relations. The designer delves into and becomes familiar with the physical, ecological, social and financial landscapes of a place. The designer, therefore, is the creative synthesizer of information.

In debilitating landscapes, the synthesis of information, fostering of relationships and facilitating of conversations between several often unrelated and even conflicting parties is crucial to the success of a project. By conducting outreach and community engagement, the designer, as synthesizer of information, invites the time, energy, skills and creativity of individuals while communicating mutual benefits and rewards.[5] Co-producers then become co-investors.

This entails not only a sensitivity toward people in place, but also a deep reading of the landscape in a given context. Anne Spirn, landscape architect and activist, working for decades in the West Philadelphia neighborhood of Mill Creek, argues that the designer's primarily role is to assist a community with reading the local landscape as a way of establishing their sense of place.[6] In Philadelphia, where one in four residents live in poverty,[7] and with nearly 40,000 vacant properties across the city,[8] the debilitating landscape is a fact of life. Spirn's years of local activism have had an impact on Mill Creek's social and ecological conscience. For example, Spirn found that the buried floodplain upon which the residents of Mill Creek lived—something more or less invisible to the community—was potentially a galvanizing social and ecological resource.[9] She explains that this act of uncovering landscape is not to deny the problems in poor neighborhoods, but to help establish identity in places so that communities can be strengthened.

"These resources are readily apparent once the observer is prepared to see them...One who assumes the city has supplanted 'nature' is not likely to see the effects of the natural processes that still shapes the landscape; another who believes the city has "degraded" nature is apt to see only pollution. Those who think that the ravaged state of a neighborhood is the natural outcome of its occupation by an isolated 'underclass' who has lived in poverty for generations, may see only devastation." [10]

Mill Creek has undergone many changes since the string of textile mills that populated the creek banks were removed and the creek was culverted. Due to the flood plain undermining foundations, Mill Creek's housing is unsafe. New public housing projects were persistently resisted, out of prejudice and fear, by residents of industrially stable neighborhoods, like Kensington and Richmond, while Philadelphia's 19th century "streetcar suburbs", like Mill Creek, accepted them.[11] The low-income, racially homogenous population of the 21st century live in the floodplain and because of the land's instability for development, they live among huge swaths of open, untraversable land and a deteriorating housing stock.

'Great' designers can, and often did get it wrong in these situations. For example, Mill Creek was once home to a Louis Kahn designed public housing campus but this development was demolished because of its deteriorated condition related to a lack of sensitivity to both the landscape and the rest of the community.[12] Spirn's approach of establishing what she referred to as 'landscape literacy' in this neighborhood gained local, national and international attention for its sensitivity to both the landscape and the community.[13] Landscape literacy as a tool for local empowerment fostered an interest in landscape projects around the neighborhood. Spirn's work in cataloguing and developing a series of landscape initiatives to replace deteriorating vacant properties was an important first step in creating a stronger identity for the Mill Creek community. Today, however, Mill Creek is not a vibrant healthy neighborhood.

The Mill Creek landscape project failed to address all of the principles in achieving spatial equity. David Harvey, geographer and writer, says that territorial social justice can only occur when (a) the needs of the population within each territory are met, (b) resources are so allocated to have beneficial effects across territories, and (c) extra resources are allocated to help overcome special difficulties stemming from the physical and social environment.[14] For Spirn's Mill Creek project, extra resources to overcome the difficulties of the floodplain took the form of community gardens, urban forests and the removal of housing in subsiding areas. Arguably, the opening up of landscape space only added further to the urban blight of this neighborhood. More importantly, there is a general lack of access to health services, food, jobs, and public transport. To use Harvey's language, Spirn's landscape literacy and garden infill projects were not enough resources to bring territorial social justice to Mill Creek. This is to point out that spatial design changes need to be integrated with more comprehensive approaches.

Modifying the vacancy and identifying the floodplain and its history is not the only form of literacy. Landscape literacy should be expanded so that the community has access to and becomes familiar with the languages of political activism, entrepreneurship and design methods. This is easier to say than do; but an expanded notion of 'design' might bring us closer to enabling landscapes that are socially, culturally and economically facilitating. As a student of design, our design pedagogy leads us to discover the social histories of a place, to identify and reuse existing resources, to find and tie connections back to municipal networks, to repurpose abundant materials, to remediate foul landscapes and to find the financial streams that support our argument. But, when looking to traditional professional design practice, this pedagogy is lost to the client-based commission. The human-centered activism and the industrious disposition is replaced with the unamenable competition entry, and an anticipation for the phone to ring.

Fortunately, there is a rich history of design practitioners breaking tradition, designing for justice, and leading from the edge. Mill Creek and Philadelphia can benefit from design tactics used in non-traditional design practice, incorporating both the spatial and non-spatial aspects of a site, and other cities dealing with comparable measures of poverty, violence and crime. VPUU, Violence Prevention through Urban Upgrading, is one such project designed to mitigate criminal activity through environmental, social and economic upgrades.

This holistic approach was funded through public and private partnership with the City of Cape Town, national and international development funds, private investors, some 28 NGOs, and local leaders of the project's site, Khayelitsha near Cape Town.[15] Tarna Klitzner, a South African landscape architect, was chosen for the ILASA award of excellence for her work on VPUU.[16] The VPUU project is a thorough investigation of the non-spatial and spatial drivers of criminal activity in Khayelitsha. Their approach identifies ways to stimulate community development, institutional involvement and economic activity through environmental upgrades of the city in the floodplain.[17]

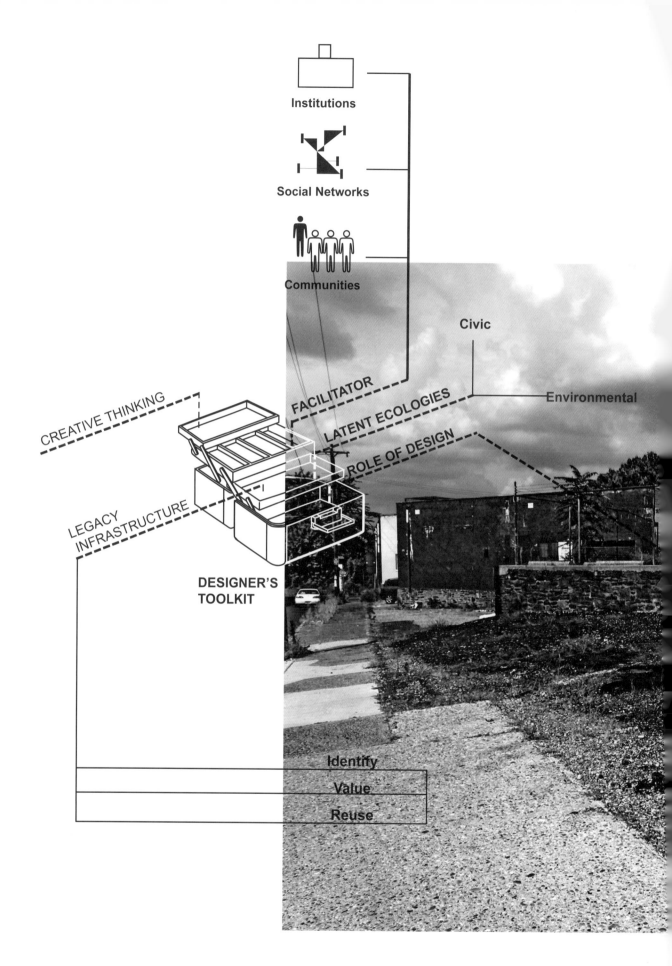

Institutions

Social Networks

Communities

Civic

Environmental

CREATIVE THINKING

FACILITATOR

LATENT ECOLOGIES

ROLE OF DESIGN

LEGACY
INFRASTRUCTURE

DESIGNER'S
TOOLKIT

Identify

Value

Reuse

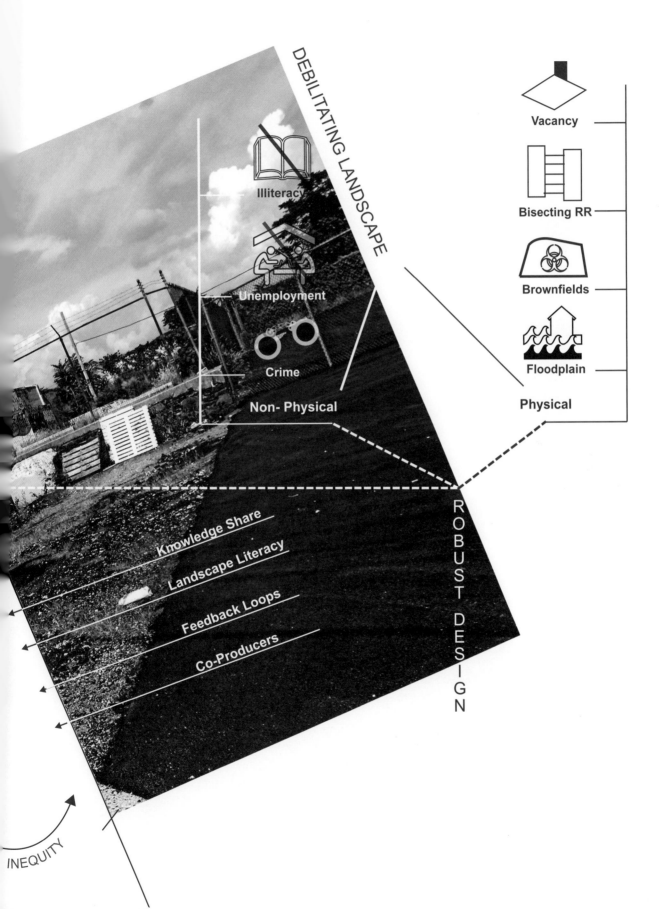

DEBILITATING LANDSCAPE

Illiteracy

Unemployment

Crime

Non- Physical

Vacancy

Bisecting RR

Brownfields

Floodplain

Physical

ROBUST DESIGN

Knowledge Share

Landscape Literacy

Feedback Loops

Co-Producers

INEQUITY

and spatial drivers of criminal activity in Khayelitsha. Their approach identifies ways to stimulate community development, institutional involvement and economic activity through environmental upgrades of the city in the floodplain.[17]

Like areas of Philadelphia, where there is a 27.5% unemployment rate, four times the national average,[18] Khayelitsha has a largely unemployed population and, also like Philadelphia, has high criminal activity. The VPUU project began by extensive on-the-ground research, identifying types of crime, where and when they were most likely to occur, and the demographics of criminals and victims. They held community workshops to better understand the perceptions of crime and to identify and map crime hotspots such as open undefined land, areas with dark corridors with blind spots and on empty transit routes. The research and synthesis of information led to the discovery of a correlation between unemployment and criminal activity: a positive relationship, for when there is less unemployment there is less crime.[19] By overlapping the crime maps with existing social activity, transit routes, and potential business hubs, the designers created a framework for their physical interventions.[20]

The program is more than a set of infrastructural moves. It is an environmental upgrade with community and institutional involvement and stewardship. This is created with better-defined boundaries that create ownership and maintenance, upgraded schoolyards and well-lit renovated parks that are available for after-hours play. It also stimulates economic growth by clustering activities in designed plazas with locally owned shops and work–live housing, providing high foot-traffic during the day and 'eyes on the street' after dark.[21]

Empty long tracts of unlit open space, in the lowest topographical areas that retain water, were magnets for theft and harassment. These transects were identified to create safer corridors with landscape and architectural moves. 'Active' boxes with elevated viewpoints to expose criminal activity and with 24-hour programming, like a radio station, became guiding landmarks along well-defined corridors. The safe corridors were paved for pedestrian access to and from regional transportation that gathered park infrastructures, water retention, play-yards

and economic hubs.[22] Aesthetics, materials and human-scale physical interventions were a way to upgrade the environmental condition while recycling materials and employing local artisanship and building techniques.[23]

Dilapidation gives the impression of areas being unowned or discarded by the community, catering to what is commonly referred to as the 'broken window syndrome'. Conversely, well-maintained areas with high foot-traffic are seen as high-risk areas for criminals and therefore are generally safer. Ergo, the VPUU design team identified maintenance as a key to a sustained safe environment, building in networks of community management structures funded by the rental of community facilities.[24]

These physical and non-physical design interventions created a facilitating landscape for the Khayelitsha community. VPUU touches on all of David Harvey's principles for social justice by developing a design action plan around the ideas of safety. The designed work–live hubs attracted new resources of both private development and public institutional services such as libraries and legal services.[25] The defined 'safe corridors' gathered communities and allowed safe travel to other parts of the city; while the environment upgrades transformed Khayelitsha's floodplain development into local amenities. The VPUU (2005) project helped to decrease Khayelitsha's murder rate by 39% within four years of its implementation and to decrease overall crime by 20% within three years.[26] The VPUU project proves that spatial interventions have non-spatial implications and designers have the capacity to incite sustainable change. Landscape architects in Philadelphia can adopt this multi-tiered approach for social justice and a re-envisioning of the city.

Design in the debilitating landscape, demands a different kind of design intelligence. Fluency and experimentation in making space must be coupled with a willingness to be political, entrepreneurial and trans-disciplinary. Expanding the scope and engaging with both physical and non-physical design, landscape architects have the opportunity to radically transform the character of a place with spatial interventions that sustain impact.

References

1 Carolyn Adams, David Bartelt, and David Elesh, Restructuring the Philadelphia Region (Philadelphia: Temple University, 2008), 31.

2 Randolph Hester, Design for Ecological Democracy (Cambridge: MIT Press, 2010), 9.

3 Ibid., 8.

4 Fritz Wagner and Roger Caves, Community Livability: Issues and Approaches to Sustaining the Well-Being of People and Communities, (New York: Routledge, 2012), 184.

5 Avery Ware, Compendium for the Civic Economy (London: Trancity Valiz, 2012), 177.

6 "West Philadelphia Landscape Project," last modified 2010 http://www.wplp.net/2011draft/projects/landscape-literacy/

7 US CENSUS 2010.

8 Lin, Jennifer, "Philadelphia Housing Authority Seeks Takers For Vacant Properties," Philly.com, June 5, 2011.

9 Anne Spirn, "Restoring Mill Creek," Landscape Research Volume 30 (2005): 50.

10 Ibid., 409.

11 John Bauman, Public Housing, Race, and Renewal: Urban Planning in Philadelphia (Philadelphia: Temple University Press, 1987), 161.

12 Patrick Kerkstra, "Crowed Cheers As Housing Project's Walls Come Down," Philly.com, November 25, 2002.

13 Anne Sprin, "Restoring Mill Creek," 407.

14 David Harvey, Social Justice and the City (Oxford: Blackwell Publishers, 1993), 101.

15 "How Citizens And Urban Design Beat Crime," last modified 2012, http://www.leekuanyewworldcityprize.com.sg/features_khayelitsha.htm.

16 "2013 Corobrik – ILASA Awards of Excellence," last modified August 2013, http://www.ilasa.co.za/awards-of-excellence/.

17 Jared Green, J, "A New Town For Khayelitsha," The Dirt, April 16, 2012, http://dirt.asla.org/2012/04/16/a-new-town-for-khayelitsha/.

18 "Crime Maps and Stats", last modified 2013, http://www.phillypolice.com/about/crime-statistics/.

19 "How Citizens And Urban Design Beat Crime".

20 Cape Town "Bid Application: Live Design Transform Life" (document presented for the World Design Designation 2014, 2013).

21 Jared Green, "A New Town For Khayelitsha".

22 Cape Town "Bid Application: Live Design Transform Life".

23 Jared Green, "A New Town For Khayelitsha".

24 Ibid.

25 Cape Town "Bid Application: Live Design Transform Life".

26 "How Citizens And Urban Design Beat Crime".

Autumn Visconti charts out new territories where landscape architecture should engage, by altering the negative connotation of climate change.

[shift]

Climax
Autumn Visconti

Our contemporary perception relates climate 'change' to the disastrous events that affect societies the most. But climate always changes. By looking beyond its negative repercussions, can climate change have constructive outcomes? This analytical narrative refers to the spatial analysis of climate change effects and how it might benefit a forward understanding of the ever-changing landscape. This starts by considering how global socio-economic agendas can correspond to climate forecasts. By anticipating change we can use it as a driving force for design and connect immediate global investment with long-term environmental protection.

The WorldRiskReport (WRR) claims that "[h]uman intervention in the global ecosystem raises the threat and increases the extent of disasters."[1] As population increases, rapid development reduces the natural resources which protect societies against climate disruption.[2] This form of human progress has become an act of leveling the landscape for quick monetary gain. Economic growth, however, has the opportunity to fund the developing infrastructure of a country while strengthening and restoring its ecological resilience. This is particularly important for developing countries which are vulnerable to the effects of climate change.

Vulnerability to climate change is classified by institutions such as the United Nations, the U.S. Department of Defense, and the Alliance Development Works, which conduct global risk assessments in tandem with population forecasts.[3] These institutions study climate change vulnerability across multiple scenarios, using criteria including geographical exposure and poverty. By these criteria, the nation-states most at risk are developing nations across the tropics.[4] If landscape architects use spatial analysis to identify areas to work in, then the need to assess the effects of the changing environment over time is critical. Computer models do this already, but landscape architects are trained to recognize how human and natural systems react to varying pressures of population growth, climate conditions, etc.

CLIMATE CHANGE VULNERABILITY
VULNERABILITY AND CLIMATE CHANGE IMPACT ASSESSMENTS ON WORLD REGIONS MADE BY UNEP FOR ADAPTATION STRATEGIES

NEXT 11 EMERGING ECONOMIES
A GLOBAL FORECAST OF EMERGING MARKETS AROUND THE WORLD

MEGA-INFRASTRUCTURE
EXISTING REGIONAL NETWORKS OF MULTIMODAL TRANSIT

003

001_INDON

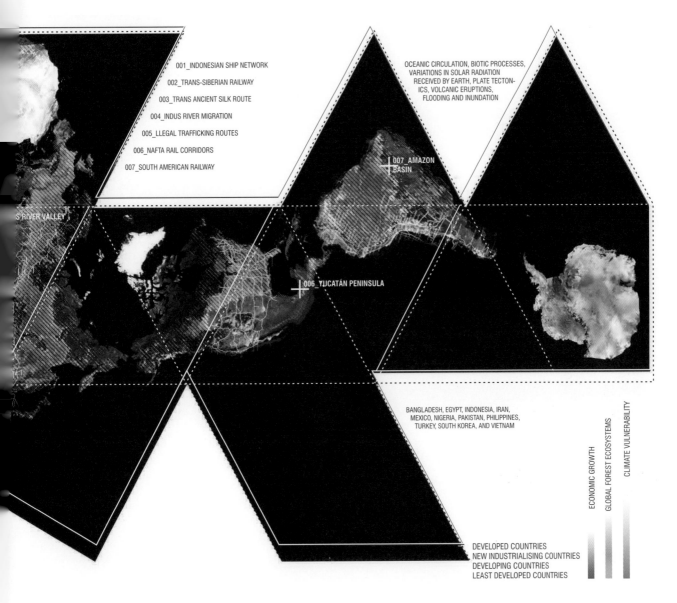

001_INDONESIAN SHIP NETWORK

002_TRANS-SIBERIAN RAILWAY

003_TRANS ANCIENT SILK ROUTE

004_INDUS RIVER MIGRATION

005_LLEGAL TRAFFICKING ROUTES

006_NAFTA RAIL CORRIDORS

007_SOUTH AMERICAN RAILWAY

OCEANIC CIRCULATION, BIOTIC PROCESSES,
VARIATIONS IN SOLAR RADIATION
RECEIVED BY EARTH, PLATE TECTON-
ICS, VOLCANIC ERUPTIONS,
FLOODING AND INUNDATION

S RIVER VALLEY

007_AMAZON
BASIN

006_YUCATÁN PENINSULA

BANGLADESH, EGYPT, INDONESIA, IRAN,
MEXICO, NIGERIA, PAKISTAN, PHILIPPINES,
TURKEY, SOUTH KOREA, AND VIETNAM

ECONOMIC GROWTH

GLOBAL FOREST ECOSYSTEMS

CLIMATE VULNERABILITY

DEVELOPED COUNTRIES
NEW INDUSTRIALISING COUNTRIES
DEVELOPING COUNTRIES
LEAST DEVELOPED COUNTRIES

We are taught to understand the fundamentals of how humans perceive and interact openly with the environment, thus recognizing the importance of health, safety and welfare in a society. We utilize seasonal variation to cultivate growth, and maximize the abundance of resources to create renewable services. By anticipating and designing for change, we offer a potentially effective and valuable skillset for the protection of developing nation-states. We extend immediate help to those in need, yet this limits us to the remedial. By advocating our skillsets as a form of economic investment, we can strengthen the integrity of our profession by engaging with global jurisdictions.

Economic planning initiatives can begin to engage with global investors by establishing long-term environmental management strategies as a means of protection from climate disruption. One step towards protecting ecosystems is recognizing the changing effects of population growth. This gives governments and communities the incentive to increase climate change preparedness in highly vulnerable areas as natural resources continue to diminish. This notion further invites landscape architectural services to engage with the larger jurisdictions of policy and economy, therefore reaffirming our potential to influence natural systems at a larger scale. It is critical to initiate this dialogue in areas highlighted by the spatial analysis of climate change vulnerability because they are interconnected to larger economies and growing populations.

Developing countries located near the equator are geographically positioned at the forefront of increased climate disruption and face imminent risk as populations continue to grow. The growth in economic interaction between these nations amplifies the wider consequences of national decisions.[5] The newly emerging economies, the "Next 11", are rapidly industrializing nation-states anticipated to grow exponentially within the global market.[6] Superimposing these nation-states over areas of terrestrial degradation, and climate change vulnerability, shows these territories are interconnected beyond geopolitical borders. Here, economics and ecology bind us in ever-tightening networks and present complex issues that can be affected by climate change. It is vital to reassess these emerging economies and their issues at a mega-regional scale.

This allows us to gauge where economic lifelines exist and where populations might go as a result to changes in the landscape. For example, as China continues to develop, new international investment opportunities are emerging elsewhere based on inexpensive resources.[7] This is particularly true in the Southeast Pacific.[8] Population and development patterns can shift in reaction to a rising or falling economy, which pressures biologically diverse landscapes across the globe.

Southeast Asia, like other tropical regions, is considered one of the major biodiversity hotspots in the world.[9] Biological hotspots are areas of exceptional concentrations of endemic species undergoing loss of habitat.[10] Over past decades, human activity and ongoing poor land management has accelerated the degradation of ecosystems. This refers to the 90% of already protected, bio-diverse areas that are soon to be impacted by future development in rapidly developing low- and moderate-income countries.[11] This is a result of an increasing economy because societies continue to diminish natural resources at unsustainable rates. For landscape architects to work effectively in these regions they must appreciate the physical landscape as a product of both political and economic conditions.

By reassessing the spatial analysis of climate effects with a growing economy, the Republic of Indonesia is of particular interest because of its rich resources, biodiversity and location. Coincidentally, Indonesia is also listed as one of the "Next 11" global economies and is considered a "frontier market" that has been gaining attention from investors worldwide.[12] Indonesia is the fourth most-populous country in the world, after China, India and the United States.[13] However, just as Indonesia is positioned to boom economically it is also particularly vulnerable to both climate change disruption due to its geographic position and high levels of poverty. Its economic position is relative to population growth and presents an upfront investment opportunity that can promote and protect ecological resiliency.

Indonesia's biodiversity structurally supports its archipelago through widespread environmental defense mechanisms. However these environmental defense mechanisms will diminish over time if proper planning is ignored.

Natural systems susceptible to frequent, abrupt, disturbance are naturally regenerative and if development practices can work within the logic of these systems then capital investments will become more secure.[14] The ability to physically shape the land and engage with the resources at hand is within the skill-set of the landscape architect.

Topographic variation between natural systems can serve communities by directing the inundation of water from a storm event to groundwater recharge zones adjacent to ecologically designated areas. Other land-oriented amenities can provide areas of economic importance the protection they need from flood or coastal storm surge with a system of adjacent land conservation tracts that act as buffers. Landscape architects also incorporate human system-based approaches into large-scale master planning schemes by engaging with local cultures, therefore reinforcing a civic infrastructure. These systems can link together and effectively strengthen ecologically sensitive areas while promoting overall resiliency. By delivering amenities to communities in need, while protecting the vested interest of the economy, we can assist in reversing the collective perception of climate change from threat to resource.

In the past decade, climate change preparedness has emerged as a new theme in urban planning. This relates to the notion of 'ecosystem services' which aims to reveal the largely unseen health and economic benefits that properly managed ecosystems presents to growing populations.[15] By further attributing value to these services, the economic benefit of up-front environmental investment can promote governance in a nation's overall development agenda. If a government can embrace the concept of ecosystem services, then they can protect vulnerable populations through local environmental stewardship.

As societies continue to grow the dynamics between economy, ecology and policy need to adjust. The trajectory of a climate-based spatial analysis, plays a critical role in adjusting these dynamics. We are now presented with new ways to conceive a network of global interactions ready for resiliency design and innovation in land-use planning strategies. In conclusion, climate change can have constructive outcomes by informing a country's overall development agenda through engaging environmental stewardship with local governance, and by further advocating the role of the landscape architect. The spatial dimension of change becomes a balance between global market economies and climate-induced resources. While we can never control our changing environment, we can shift our contemporary perception of climate change, from a threat to a catalyst of positive outcomes. In doing so, we acknowledge the changing state of the land and protect its resources while fundamentally investing in the future.

References

1 Alliance Development Works, "WorldRiskReport 2012: Environmental degradation increases disaster risk worldwide," from a report presented by the United Nations University Institute for Environment and Human Security (UNU-EHS), the Alliance Development Works/Bündnis Entwicklung Hilft and The Nature Conservancy (TNC) (Brussels: Alliance Development Works/ Bündnis Entwicklung Hilft, 2012), 6.

2 Ibid, 6, 22.

3 See, United Nations Human Settlements Programme (UN-HABITAT), Global Report on Human Settlements 2011: Cities and Climate Change (London; Washington D.C.: EARTHSCAN, 2011), 1-4; Department of Defense (DoD), "Department of Defense FY 2012 Climate Change Adaptation Roadmap," Executive Order 13514 (Washington, D.C.: The United States Department of Defense (DoD), 2011), 9.

4 Alliance Development Works, "WorldRiskReport 2012: Environmental degradation increases disaster risk worldwide," from a report presented by the United Nations University Institute for Environment and Human Security (UNU-EHS), the Alliance Development Works/Bündnis Entwicklung Hilft and The Nature Conservancy (TNC) (Brussels: Alliance Development Works/ Bündnis Entwicklung Hilft, 2012), 6–12.

5 UN Documents, "Our Common Future, Chapter 1: A Threatened Future," From A/42/427. Our Common Future: Report of the World Commission on Environment and Development, http://www.un-documents.net/ocf-01.htm (accessed 11 Nov. 2013).

6 Jim O'Neil, Goldman Sachs Group Incorporated, "Beyond the BRICS: A Look at the 'Next 11'" in The Growth Map: Economic Opportunity in the BRICs and Beyond. (New York: Portfolio/ Penguin Group, 2011), 1–4.

7 "Indonesia's Economy Is Surging Forward, but Challenges Abound", University of Pennsylvania, Wharton, last modified 06/01/12, http:// knowledge.wharton.upenn.edu/article.cfm?articleid=3025 (accessed 01 Aug 2013).

8 Ibid.

9 Burak Güneralp, Robert I. McDonald, Michail Fragkias, Julie Goodness, Peter J. Marcotullio, and Karen C. Seto, "Urbanization Forecasts, Effects of Land Use, Biodiversity, and Ecosystem Services" in Urbanization, Biodiversity and Ecosystem Services: Challenges and Opportunities: A Global Assessment (Dordrecht; Heidelberg; New York; London: 2013), 443–5.

10 Norman Myers, Russell A. Mittermeier, Christina G. Mittermeier, Gustavo A.B. da Fonseca and Jennifer Kent, "Biodiversity Hotspots for Conservation Priorities," Nature 403 (2000): 853.

11 Karen C. Seto, Susan Parnell, and Thomas Elmqvist, "A Global outlook on Urbanization," in Urbanization, Biodiversity and Ecosystem Services: Challenges and Opportunities: A Global Assessment (Dordrecht; Heidelberg; New York; London: 2013), 8.

12 Wasatch Funds, "Frontier Markets and Emerging Small Countries: Elements of an Emerging Asset Class," (Economic Dataset, ALPS Distributors, Inc., 2012), 2, 9.

13 The CIA World Fact Book, East & Southeast Asia: Indonesia (2013). https://www.cia.gov/library/publications/the-world-factbook/geos/id.html (accessed 25 Sept 2013).

14 Lance Gunderson, "Ecological and Human Community Resilience in Response to Natural Disasters." Ecology and Society 15, No. 2 (2010): 18.

15 Cities and Biodiversity Outlook Project, "A Global Outlook on Urbanization," in Urbanization, Biodiversity and Ecosystem Services: Challenges and Opportunities (Dordrecht Heidelberg New York London: Springer, 2013), Vi-10.

Through a memoir and analysis, Suzanne Mahoney explores the Aokihagara Forest and its culture of suicide.

[death]

555-22-0110

Suzanne Mahoney

It's 14 square miles and has about 10 miles of known trail. I walked every inch of those trails and found nothing at first. It's great for bird watching, if you're into that kind of thing. The bus will drop you off right in front of the bird sanctuary or at one of the three caves. There is the Bat Cave with cheesy Batman figurines everywhere. Then there is the Ice Cave with glowing blue ice (the ice is only blue because there is a giant blue spotlight on it). And lastly, there is the Lava Cave with slimy cramped spaces just like the other two caves. The caves are cool, I guess, but mostly a tourist trap. I didn't come here to see the caves.

The caves and surrounding area were formed from the lava of the neighboring volcano. I climbed the mountain during the night to see the sunrise from the summit. Weak from altitude sickness, I collapsed at the top just as the sun burst through the haze, then I cried. The view was the most beautiful thing I'd ever seen, but I didn't come here for the view.

I flew 15 hours east to see a forest. I know very little about forests, ecosystems, or even trees for that matter. I don't have much experience hiking or camping. Would I get lost? I heard from a friend that compasses don't even work in there. Good thing I bought colored tape to mark my path. The first half-mile of the forest is covered in colored tape, which I intended to follow.

I got off the bus at the Lava Cave. There were two vehicles parked at the forest entrance with four patrol rangers waiting. As I made my way closer to the entrance one ranger tried to initiate a conversation with me, but all I could say was hello since I don't speak the language. I passed the surveillance camera and entered the forest. I walked for about 20 minutes and then came to a fork in the trail so I went right, in the direction of the mountain. I finally found the place: roped off and marked "no entry". I had seen images of this sign online so I knew this was the way. I crossed over the ropes and went through. Although off-trail, the path was well worn and there were layers of old tape almost immediately, embedded in the ground and on some trees. On either side I could see faint lines of tape in the distance, but I stayed on the worn path.

I walked for a bit and saw a fire pit in the middle of the path. The stones were blackened, looking recently used with leftover trash in the center. Then I noticed the skull, just resting there on the side of the trail bank. It was so out of place. No other remnants were around this skull. It must have been moved from its original place in the forest. Moved, not to warn people of what lies out there, but to fulfill the spectator's desire to see evidence of death. So, as a spectator I took my picture and kept moving.

As I continued to walk further along this main trail, I saw a blur of blue to my right. I knew it was more than just colored tape in the distance. I pulled out my own red tape to mark my path as I went off trail. The blue was a tarp covering a tent. In front of the tent was a mangled skeleton with debris all around. I recognized parts of the site from pictures online. Just like the first skull, I felt that something wasn't right. Was this skeleton a fake? Am I on some hidden camera show? So, as a contestant I took my picture and kept moving.

Following my own tape back to the worn trail, I continued looking for tape that went off course. I followed one line of tape to reach a pair of nooses hanging from a single tree. I only noticed these from the bright pink robe that lay limp beneath. This was the first finding that felt real. There were no human remains, no images of this online that I had seen, nothing stage like, just some rope and clothing in the middle of this vast forest. It hit me: someone died here. At this exact spot, someone took their own life. What would it take for me, for you, to end your life, to decide not to live anymore? I've had days where living is hard work — faking the smile, acting like I'm okay, but hating myself to the point where death seems...better. I've been there, at that point, but I was never willing to end it all. How could she do that? There had to be something to look forward to, some hope, some love, some thing. We all need something to get us through and she didn't have that.

Pushing through the sadness of what I'd just seen, I followed several other lines of tape which led to nothing more then a few beer cans. So I called it a day. I got my five dollars worth; I saw a real skeleton in the suicide forest. I left the forest through the same entrance, greeted by the same four men I saw on my way into the forest. One man jumped out of the car and handed me two pieces of candy. I actually think they were happier to see me come out of the forest than I was. I was one less body to search for in there. The candy was disgusting so I treated myself to ice cream at the Lava Cave gift shop. Perhaps they should incentivize everyone to return from the forest with candy and ice cream.

- Suzanne

As a set, the Aokigahara Forest contains various
found evidence which can be overlaid to reveal
own narratives. A catalogue of imagery includes
ents of signage, wildlife, tape, formation
Spectators are encouraged to
where do

This investigation of the Aokigahara Forest was initiated as a means to understand the notorious phenomena of suicide within this sacred Japanese forest. Focus was centered on the unknown narratives of suicide victims and how these narratives leave a physical mark on the forest itself. These marks or residual evidence (tape, discarded clothing, human decay) can then be traced to assemble a narrative of suicide. Further research and firsthand experience diverted this topic to one of human experience and perception of landscapes. The suicide forest is an example of how natural landscapes have become simulations.

N. Katherine Hayles describes simulated landscapes in her article *Simulated Nature and Natural Simulations: Rethinking the Relation between the Beholder and the World*:

> "When 'nature' becomes an object for visual consumption, to be appreciated by the connoisseur's eye sweeping over an expanse of landscape, there is a good chance it has already left the realm of firsthand experience and entered the category of constructed experience that we can appropriately call simulation." [1]

Un-designed landscapes, known as First Nature, are actually simulations designed through media and human histories. Through design in the form of online blogs, photos, videos, maps, and guidebooks, spectators are able to experience the Aokigahara Forest without ever visiting. Firsthand experiences in the forest are tainted by this prior knowledge leaving very little left to discover in "the wild". With no limit to design, humans have effectively tamed First Nature and in the case of the Aokigahara Forest, the media "trash" has inadvertently affected the forest, bringing ghost-hunters, thrill seekers, scavengers, surveillance cameras, and a suicide patrol unit into this once peaceful place.

The Complete Manual of Suicide by Wataru Tsurumi (often found within the forest) describes the Aokigahara Forest as the perfect place to die for its quiet seclusion, but this can no longer be true. The forest has lost the sense of sacredness as a retreat from the pressures of Japanese culture. Victims who choose the forest as a place to die will be found and their deaths will be scrutinized just as those of victims who choose a high-speed train station, another popular place for suicide in Japan. There are implied differences

between train stations and the forest and the narratives of those who commit suicide at either. Japanese train stations operate like machines reflecting the strict order and high expectations of Japanese culture. There is a consistent flow of human traffic set to the precise schedule of the trains. Daily commuters run on autopilot transferring trains from point A to point B without a second thought. Considering suicide in a place like this seems similar to the autopilot mechanics of the stations. You pick a train: a train that you know will be exactly on time as most trains are in Japan. The act is instantaneous, over in seconds. This act is public, losing all sense of privacy and sensitivity just as the stations themselves are designed. Train schedules are delayed following a suicide on the tracks and families of the victim are charged for cleanup fees. Suicides in Japanese train stations have become routine and banal and thus disconnected from the deeply personal act that is suicide.

To choose the forest as your final place on earth requires a very different mentality than choosing a train station. Entering the forest with intentions of suicide reflects Man's desire to return to First Nature. This may be especially relevant to the Japanese view of First Nature discussed by Hubertus Tellenbach and Bin Kimura:

> "...they [Japanese] apprehend Onozumara and Mizukara, nature and self, as originating from the same common ground... In expressing the common ground of Onozumara and Mizukara, nature and self, the Japanese thus point to something like a spontaneous becoming, a force flowing forth from an original source. [2]

As described by Japanese language, human instinct, it seems, is to reconnect with Nature or Oneself. The forest offered Japanese people that opportunity as a place of contemplation and ultimately oneness with Nature through death. This is not a place one passes each day on a daily commute. Traveling to the forest requires intention and preparedness. Equipment such as a rope or sleeping pills must be obtained and brought with you. And the final act is completed alone. There is no train conductor or high-speed train that can carry this out for you. You must tie the rope and you must count the pills. A suicide in the forest therefore requires more contemplation. Some choose to camp out in the forest for days resolving whether or not to end their lives. Others thread colored tape around trees to mark their

path through the forest as a means to find their way out if they choose not to commit suicide. The Suicide Patrol follows the threads of tape to collect the bodies. Ghost hunters and thrill seekers do the same equipped with video cameras and intentions to exploit the phenomenon. All reverence has been lost in the forest.

"It was quiet. She stood there, looking at the lake. The opposite side was brown lava, on top of it: the sea of trees, which spread endlessly towards the bottom like an ocean."[3] Initially romanticized through novels such as Matsumoto Seicho's *Tower of Wave,* suicide in this forest now exposes the harsh realities of the suicide culture in Japan pointing directly to societal pressures in a highly constructed environment. Through interference of design, the Aokigahara Forest has become equivalent to the hyper-designed train stations. They are both stage sets, places to observe suicide as a cultural phenomenon. Death is objectified and consumed by media spectators. As the forest is continuously advertized through media, Japanese perceived tolerance of suicide may shift. Either new suicide refuges will be sought or perhaps cultural and societal dynamics will adjust.

Your life is a precious gift from your parents.
Think about them and the rest of your family.
You don't have to suffer alone.
Call us. 555-22-0110

References

1 N. Katherine Hayles, Simulated Nature and Natural Simulations: Rethinking the Relation between the Beholder and the World (New York: W.W. Norton & Company, 1996), 411.

2 Hubertus Tellenbach and Bin Kimura, The Japanese Concept of "Nature" (Albany: State University of New York Press, 1989), 154

3 Pejik Malinovski, David Spalding Sharp, and Kurt Anderson, Suicide Forest (Idlewood Recordings, 2010) Web.

In this review of Andres Duany's "Landscape Urbanism and its Discontents", Diana Gruberg and Ian Sinclair provide a response that studies cities as incomplete phenomena.

[review]

Unfinished Cities
(And Incomplete Theories)
Diana Gruberg & Ian Sinclair

Incomplete Theories

As designers, we are interested not only in the tools of site and city design, but also the ideologies that impact the construction of urban form. From Modernism to City Beautiful, to urban renewal and environmental planning, we must sift through a broad range of urban design theories as we formulate our own design ethics. We learn about the successes and failures of many design and planning strategies, and how a city endures despite constant disturbance. Responding to de-industrialization and patterns of urbanization in the United States, a number of approaches have emerged in the past 30 years that address the decline of urban centers and the emergence of suburban sprawl.

A recent collection of essays, *Landscape Urbanism and its Discontents: Dissimulating the Sustainable City,* presents a debate between two predominant urban design philosophies: New Urbanism and landscape urbanism. New Urbanism has gained traction since the 1980s as a form driven and practice-based approach to city planning, while landscape urbanism emerged in the late 1990s as a loosely defined academic theory that aims to expand the definition of landscape and to design urban processes through this broader conception. The book is characterized most noticeably by its antagonism towards landscape urbanism, and "turf warfare" has been central to both the book's writing and reception.[1] The essays range from pejorative and polemical, to apologetic and descriptive, to critical and thought provoking. Arguments revolve around one or more of the following topics: defining "the city" and its constituent parts; the ethics of urban design; the relationship between "man" and "nature;" and the relationship between "art" and "life." This broad scope of topics spans more than the volume can sufficiently manage.

Edited by Andrés Duany and Emily Talen, both prominent New Urbanists, *Landscape Urbanism and its Discontents* aims to address what they view as the "differing visions of nature and society"[2] advocated by landscape urbanism and New Urbanism. For the editors, landscape urbanism lacks a sound moral foundation, a result of top-down design that belies place. They claim efficacy for New Urbanism's design principles, and moral high ground for its social agenda. Interestingly, landscape urbanism lacks concise definition even by its most prominent thinkers and practitioners. Richard Weller's 2006 appraisal of landscape urbanism as a "fuzzy cluster of rhetorical positioning"[3] is arguably still true today. Landscape urbanism's intellectual disorganization is in stark contrast to the unambiguous principles and institutional structure of the Congress for the New Urbanism. The relative incoherence of landscape urbanism allows the book's authors to actively define the subject through their assessment.

On Sustainability

Discontents posits a twofold critique of landscape urbanism, claiming it is not ecologically sustainable and that it lacks a coherent social agenda. On the topic of sustainability, the book makes three main arguments: landscape urbanist projects tacitly embrace sprawl; they lack sound scientific criteria and empirical evidence as the basis for design interventions; and their use of cloudy language evades conventional frameworks for evaluation.

According to New Urbanist doctrine, low-density development is inherently unsustainable, a concept Andrés Duany, Douglas Kelbaugh, and Paul Murrain elaborate upon in their respective articles. Kelbaugh praises New Urbanism's emphasis on specific physical aspects of cities, which he calls the "urbanistically spatial."[4] Formal elements include "compact, complete communities"[5] and "the high, straight street wall of buildings"[6] as well as "the gridded, as opposed to the dendritic, network of streets."[7] Such attributes, according to Kelbaugh, make them better both as social centers and in reducing their global carbon footprint. A number of authors extend this argument to a holistic idea that the built and the natural environments must remain separate. This principle, which forms the basis for Duany's urban-to-rural transect,[8] appears to be absolute.

New Urbanism's fundamentalism undermines its pragmatism. If we are always starting from scratch in designing cities, it makes sense to concentrate density in particular areas. However, initial conditions are critical. In cities that have experienced rapid de-industrialization and de-population, for example, the remaining population is typically spread out across a large area. The New Urbanists have no easy solution to re-invent these urban areas. While they argue that landscape urbanism's design principles should be based on measurable scientific criteria such as carbon emissions and energy use, it is not always clear that these are appropriate forms of measurement. In shrinking cities, there are many other variables, including the costs of uprooting populations, providing employment and clearing large swaths of land, which must be taken into account. The route to sustainability is not necessarily obvious.

Michael Rios, Kristina Hill and Larissa Larsen, Jusuck Koh, and Perry Pei-Ju Yang, take less aggressive positions than others, claiming that while the measurable environmental benefits of high density are obvious, natural and civic systems are not mutually exclusive. In this vein, Hill and Larsen commend landscape urbanism for prioritizing ecosystem services and watersheds as much as city blocks.[9] They also sensibly observe, however, that landscape urbanism's use of obfuscating language masks the potential of its ideas.[10] Consider the following quote from Charles Waldheim in the *Landscape Urbanism Reader:*

> "Across a range of disciplines, many authors have articulated this newfound relevance of landscape in describing the temporal mutability and horizontal extensivity of the contemporary city."[11]

We agree that the 21st century city requires different tools and techniques, especially in the face of de-population, sprawl, and climate change, but vague language impedes productive discussion by evading the types of boundaries that could support evaluation. As Hill and Larsen note, landscape urbanists seem to eschew the "progressive construction of theory via hypothesis-testing"[12] that can inform intelligent design decisions.

On Social Agendas

The social critique offered by *Discontents* includes three distinct arguments: heroic artistic expression obstructs grassroots populism; conceptual experimentation produces socially apathetic design; and landscape urbanism's social agenda is incomplete because it fails to effectively integrate ecological and social problems.

In "Art Vitiating Life", Michael Mehaffy asserts that the individualistic act of an artist's "will-to-making" is a threat to populist forms of city making. He claims that art, as manifested in the work of landscape urbanists and other 20th century urban designers, threatens to impose itself on the city in a "totalizing and life-damaging way."[13] His oppositional dialectic between art and life is disturbing. Calling forth Jane Jacobs, Mehaffy offers an alternative model to landscape urbanism's "impoverished and tokenistic program,"[14] that would tap into what he refers to as the "evolutionary recurrence" of human activities inherent to the city.[15] The reader is left with a narrow view of "art" without a deeper understanding of how aesthetics can shape and embody social values, or how populist art might mediate between the individual and collective. Conclusions are founded in the same circular reasoning that they correctly identify with landscape urbanist writing.

In perhaps the most acerbic social critique of the book, Emily Talen argues that landscape urbanism's social agenda is disingenuous. She says that in evoking both ecology and Marxism, landscape urbanists create an elaborate guise for "value-free experimentation" made possible by neo-liberal capitalism.[16] She bemoans landscape urbanists' social indifference, a kind of apathy made more insidious by their revolutionary pretext. Talen's disgust is loud and clear: "With the intellectual cover of ecology and Marxism, infused with post-structuralist pomp, they are able to offer up a revolution in city-making."[17] In her apparent horror, she fails to address the difficulty urban design projects have faced in equitably augmenting social justice. Design philosophies, her approach included, inevitably involve contradictions in rhetoric and practice.

Michael Rios achieves a more nuanced social critique. He argues that landscape urbanism favors ecological over social representation in cities, thus neglecting the most marginalized sectors of society. He praises New Urbanism for articulating a "civic purpose of urban design" but reproaches both for failing to adequately address social inequality. He calls for a "social ecology of urbanism," which recognizes that "ecological problems are deeply social in nature and cannot be separated from larger political and social dynamics."[18] Indictments on how environmental interventions have social implications, including the kind Anne Whiston Spirn has posited in her analysis of Mill Creek in Philadelphia[19] have potential to tackle issues in ways that transcend the debate between "isms."[20]

Unfinished Cities

If nothing else, the feud between the two approaches demonstrates the capacities and limits of each. New Urbanism's empirically derived code includes a thorough range of specific forms designed to achieve prescribed urban goals and experiences. However, exclusively formal strategies often neglect new input, and freeze the environment in a particular historical and cultural context. By observing particular aspects of the built environment and applying them universally, New Urbanist development patterns cannot account for many changing aspects of contemporary life. On the other side of the coin, "process," essential to the landscape urbanism, can open up the city to new kinds of engagement, understanding and use. Designing through processes might allow for more nuance, greater variable range and help the designed place adapt to changing contexts. Still, an exclusive focus on natural processes can encourage designers to propose a project in time scales far beyond human life, potentially ignoring stakeholders and creating unrealistic expectations.[21] As Milton Curry reminds us, "We always need a social analysis of form just as we need for form to provocate analysis of the social."[22]

At times an effective strategy, the promotion of "universal typologies,"[23] whether form-derived or process-based, is problematic. Because of this, urban designers would do well to define their ethics and design strategies in terms of specific circumstances and potential effectiveness. Such an approach might waylay the impulse to laud the infallibility of a "universal" code or to claim the primacy of a mode of thinking in the absence of practical inquiry. Hill and Larsen's piece acknowledges these limits, which remain relevant to all designers:

> "[B]y acknowledging that design can't solve larger structural injustices, New Urbanists must temper their expansive claims. Duany once stated his belief in, 'the ability of architecture to transform society.' This statement exaggerates the power of physical design, neglects the darker, potentially exclusionary side of community, and undercuts New Urbanism's positive contributions."[24]

This candid reflection is a welcome pause in a book that is often unnecessarily confrontational. Despite some insightful moments, the bluster peppered throughout *Discontents* reduces city design to ideological debate and clouds a fundamental paradox that designers of cities must face. Progressive designers claim to "do good" in the city through an engagement with major instruments of change – more equitable living conditions, access to amenity and thoughtfully designed public space. But they must simultaneously recognize a plurality of values, the range of means available to achieve them, and the limits of urban design in the larger projects of social and environmental justice. As is raised by many authors in the book, landscape urbanism is not a sufficient model for urbanism. Neither, for that matter, is New Urbanism. Each approach aspires to do more than it can, and by claiming superior relevance or special knowledge, each inflates its design principles to the point of worldview. Engaging particular aspects of the city and its stakeholders, rather than totalizing theories of its mechanisms, might allow designers with differing philosophies to transcend ideological boundaries and engage problems collectively.

References

1 See Michael Sorkin."Rumble in the Jungle," Architectural Record, (August 2013) and Emily Talen's and Andrés Duany's response in Architectural Record, August 2013.

2 Andrés Duany and Emily Talen, "Looking Backward: Notes on a Cultural Episode," in Landscape Urbanism and Its Discontents, ed. Andrés Duany and Emily Talen (Gabriola Island, Canada: New Society Publishers, 2013) 3.

3 Richard Weller. "An Art of Instrumentality: Thinking Through Landscape Urbanism" in The Landscape Urbanism Reader (Princeton, NJ: Princeton Architectural Press, 2006), 71.

4 Dougals Kelbaugh, "Landscape Urbanism, New Urbanism, and the Environmental Paradox of Cities," Landscape Urbanism and its Discontents, ed. Andrés Duany and Emily Talen (Gabriola Island, Canada: New Society Publishers, 2013), 71.

5 Ibid., 70.

6 Ibid., 71.

7 Ibid., 66.

8 The urban-to-rural transect is a planning concept developed by Andrés Duany, originally created as an alternative to Euclidean zoning. It establishes six formal development types for an idealized city, from the most rural to the densest urban, and is focused on pedestrian accessibility, neighborhood identity, and the concept of defensible space. It is an important foundational concept for smart growth proponents, The Congress of New Urbanism, and Duany Plater-Zyberk & Company's SmartCode.

9 Kristina Hill and Larissa Larsen, "Adaptive Urbanism," Landscape Urbanism and its Discontents, ed. Andrés Duany and Emily Talen (Gabriola Island, Canada: New Society Publishers, 2013), 219.

10 Ibid.

11 Charles Waldheim. "An Art of Instrumentality: Thinking Through Landscape Urbanism" in The Landscape Urbanism Reader (Princeton, NJ: Princeton Architectural Press, 2006) 37.

12 Hill and Larsen, 223.

13 Michael Mehaffy. "Art Vitiating Life," Landscape Urbanism and its Discontents, ed. Andrés Duany and Emily Talen (Gabriola Island, Canada: New Society Publishers, 2013), 187.

14 Ibid., 196.

15 Ibid., 195.

16 Emily Talen, "The Social Apathy of Landscape Urbanism," Landscape Urbanism and its Discontents, ed. Andrés Duany and Emily Talen (Gabriola Island, Canada: New Society Publishers, 2013), 108.

17 Ibid., 113.

18 Michael Rios, "Marginality and the Prospect for Urbanism in the Post-Ecological City," Landscape Urbanism and its Discontents, ed. Andrés Duany and Emily Talen (Gabriola Island, Canada: New Society Publishers, 2013), 208

19 See Anne Whiston Spirn, "Restoring Mill Creek: Landscape Literacy, Environmental Justice and City Planning and Design," Landscape Research, Vol. 30, No. 3 (July 2005): 395–413.

20 Scott Page, "Planning 'isms'," Design Advocacy Group, May 2011, http://www.designadvocacy. org/dagspace/planning-"isms"/.

21 See Yates Mckee's critique of post-Katrina design competitions for New Orleans in "Haunted Housing: Eco-Vangaurdism, Eviction, and the Biopolitics of Sustainability," Grey Room 30. (March 2008): 84–113

22 Milton Curry, "Racial Critique of Public Housing Redevelopment Strategies," Suburban Sprawl: Culture, Theory, and Politics, ed. Hugh Bartling and Matthew J. Lindstrom (Washington, D.C.: Rowman and Littlefield, 2003), 128.

23 Kelbaugh, 76.

24 Hill and Larsen, 218.

[image credits]

[cover]
cover image - The World is a Rorschach Stain - Courtesy: Leonardo Robleto Costante

[editorial]
pg. 6 - Nauru Satellite, May 5th, 2005 - Courtesy: U.S. Department of Energy's Atmospheric Radiation Measurement Program

[wild]
pg. 8-9 - Image - Courtesy: Ashley M Braquet
pg. 14-15 - Fig. 1 - Courtesy: Claire Hoch

[reveal]
pg. 18-19 - Image - Courtesy: Barrett Doherty
pg. 21 - Fig. 1 -Courtesy: Matthew Wiener
pg. 24-25 - Fig. 2 -Courtesy: Matthew Wiener

[consume]
pg. 28-29 - Image - Courtesy: Leonardo Robleto Costante
pg. 33 - Fig. 1 -Courtesy: Janet Lee + Kuhn Lee

[waste]
pg. 36-37 - Image - Courtesy: Barrett Doherty
pg. 39 - Fig.1 - Courtesy: Alyssa Olson
pg. 41 - Fig.2 - Courtesy: Alyssa Olson
pg. 42 - Fig.3 - Courtesy: Alyssa Olson
pg. 43 - Fig.4 - Courtesy: Alyssa Olson
pg. 44-45 - Fig.5 - Courtesy: Alyssa Olson

[grow]
pg.46-47 - Image - Courtesy: Youngsoo Kim
pg. 48 - Image - Courtesy: Youngsoo Kim
pg. 50-51 - Image - Courtesy: Youngsoo Kim
pg. 52 - Image - Courtesy: Youngsoo Kim

[unearth]
pg. 54-55 - Image - Courtesy: Barrett Doherty
pg.56 - Image © 2013 TerraMetrics
pg.58 - Images © 2013 TerraMetrics
pg. 60-61 - Fig.1 - Courtesy: Michael Ockrant Shafir
pg. 62 - Images © 2013 TerraMetrics

[rise]
pg. 64-65 - Image - Courtesy: Barrett Doherty
pg. 66 - Fig.1 - Courtesy: Joanna Karaman
pg. 69 - Fig.2-3 - Courtesy: Joanna Karaman
pg. 70-71 - Fig.4-5 - Courtesy: Joanna Karaman
pg. 72 - Fig.6 - Courtesy: Joanna Karaman

[extract]
pg. 74-75 - Image - Courtesy: Ashley M Braquet
pg. 80 - Fig. 1 - Courtesy: Anneliza Carmalt Kauffer

[empower]
pg. 84-85 - Image - Courtesy: Barrett Doherty
pg. 87 - Fig. 1 - Courtesy: Anooshey Rahim and Helen Yu
pg. 90-91 - Fig. 2 - 3 - Courtesy: Anooshey Rahim

[shift]
pg.94-95 - Image -Courtesy: Leonardo Robleto Costante
pg. 96-97 - Fig. 1 - Courtesy: Autumn Visconti
pg. 98 - Fig. 2 - Courtesy: Autumn Visconti
pg. 100-101 - Fig. 3 - Courtesy: Autumn Visconti

[death]
pg. 104-105 - Image - Courtesy: Suzanne Mahoney
pg. 108-109 - Fig. 1 - Courtesy: Suzanne Mahoney
pg. 111 - Fig. 2 - 4 - Courtesy: Suzanne Mahoney

[review]
pg. 114-115 - Courtesy: Leonardo Robleto Costante

The creative directors of Landscapes of [Sub]stance would like to thank the authors and contributors: Anneliza Carmalt Kaufer, Diana Gruberg, Claire Hoch, Joanna Karaman, Youngsoo Kim, Janet Lee, Kuhn Lee, Suzanne Mahoney, Alyssa Olson, Anooshey Rahim, Michael Shafir, Ian Sinclair, Autumn Visconti, and Matthew Wiener.

Thanks to Barrett Doherty for providing images used in introducing the individual author pieces. Special thanks to Darcy Van Burskirk and Diane Pringle for their administrative support and patience in assisting issues related to the publication. Thanks to Gordon Goff, Usana Shadday, Alexandria Nazar and the team at ORO for their enthusiastic insight and support for the journal.

Thanks to Roslyn Shafir and Steven Ockrant for their generous support and contribution.

Finally, special thanks to Richard Weller who has supported and instigated the project through several conversations, edits and iterations and to Tatum Hands for editorial expertise and feedback throughout the process.

- Landscapes of [Sub]stance Creative Directors
Ashley Braquet, Leonardo Robleto Costante and Eduardo Santamaria Ruvalcaba